Leadership Through Learning Program

011 Award for Excellence in Program Innovation nd Design for Lifelong Learning

MHA Institute offers certified Leadership & Practitioner Development Programs

These unique programs use an integrated set of diagnostic and learning approaches, focusing on ways of thinking and acting that create emergent leaders and learning organizations.

leaders . teams . practitioners

To deal with the conditions that change creates, people in organizations use all of the skills, knowledge, and experience that they have at their disposal. In today's complex environment, people often find that their solutions to problems do not work over the long term, or that their fixes actually cause more problems to appear. As a result, people are often frustrated and confused, asking themselves, "Why do our fixes not work? What are we doing wrong? Why can't we make things better?" Adding to the complexity is the belief that there never seems to be enough resources or time to adequately address the problems.

Unless people in organizations can learn to think and act differently, they will continue to struggle with problems they cannot seem to solve. If organizations are to match the speed of change, people need completely different approaches to dealing with complexity. The MHA Institute Leadership Through Learning (LTL) Program features these approaches — ways of thinking and acting that enable everyone in an organization to solve real problems in real time, and to create the resilience required to deal with complexity and change. The LTL Program integrates an action learning approach with a decision support system; these strategies work together to help leaders make informed decisions and take effective actions in real time.

Target Audience

The LTL Program focuses on developing skills in:

- ☐ Those currently in leadership positions

- ☐ Those who aspire to leadership positions

- ☐ Teams who wish to become high performing

- ☐ Those currently in practitioner positions such as internal or external consultants

- ☐ Those who aspire to be a practitioner

Objectives

The LTL Program uses:

- Ways of thinking and learning that assist you to understand and deal with increasing complexity, change, and uncertainty

- A decision support system that assists you to thrive in conditions of increasing complexity, change, and uncertainty

- Learning within an action learning community in which you apply your learning to your own specific real-life situations.

In the LTL Program, you experience what it means to become an expert learner and emergent leader by learning in action within collaborative communities of practice using the action learning process. Action learning is a process by which new knowledge is created. In order to produce new knowledge, you will engage in the action learning process. As a result, you become an expert learner who does not give up when the going gets tough. The LTL Program creates the conditions in which expert learners develop and thrive.

As a result of completing the LTL Program, you will be able to:

- Generate the knowledge required to anticipate and to create the possibility of multiple futures

- Take the initiative to identify problems at your level, and to solve those problems in sustainable ways

- Create a culture that favours conversation and inquiry, and shared ownership of both the problem and the solution to the problem

- Create and sustain a high level of internal motivation

- Learn continuously with others, in order to develop the skills and capabilities to design and implement your own learning systems

- Release your talent and energy for innovation, creativity, and risk

- Increase your capacity to understand others, your ability to achieve results in spite of uncertainty, and your ability to work with diverse people and groups

- Embrace complexity, uncertainty, change, and diversity, so that you can anticipate and respond effectively to any change or circumstance

Leadership Through Learning Program

There are seven courses in the MHA Institute Leadership Through Learning Development Program; each course is three days in length. The entire program is usually completed in about 18 months.

Course Name	Course Description
Learning Styles: Revving Up Thinking and Learning  **Guide:** *Revving Up Thinking and Learning: Course Design Guide* **Learning Organization Disciplines:** Personal Mastery, Mental Models and Shared Vision	Examine learning styles, thinking styles, and facilitating styles, in order to understand how to design for learning. Discover how to engage even the most resistant learner. As a result, you are able to use the action learning design system to create learning interventions, courses and programs that foster emergent leadership.
Action Learning: Solving Real Problems in Real Time **Guide:** *Solving Real Problems in Real Time: Action Learning Guide* **Learning Organization Disciplines:** Personal Mastery and Team Learning	Examine workplace situations using an action learning process that focuses on people learning in collaboration by solving real problems in the workplace in real time. As a result, you are able to conduct action learning experiences with others.
System Thinking : Navigating Through Complexity **Guide:** *Navigating Through Complexity: System Thinking Guide* **Learning Organization Disciplines:** System Thinking and Mental Models	Examine workplace situations from an operational perspective in which all aspects of the work being done are considered as part of a larger and more complex system. Examples include dealing effectively with recurring problems, the effect of time delay, and scenario planning. As a result, you are able to conduct systems thinking experiences with others.
Reflexive Practice: Living with Complexity, Relationships, and Strange Loops **Guide:** *Complexity, Relationships, and Strange Loops: Reflexive Practice Guide*  **Learning Organization Disciplines:** Mental Models, Systems Thinking and Personal Mastery	Examine workplace situations from a relational perspective in which fears, anxieties, expectations, and hopes create patterns of action that are often ineffective in the workplace. Examples include people displaying unpredictable and/or difficult patterns of behaviour. As a result, you are able to conduct reflexive practice experiences with others.

Course Name	Course Description
Strategic Practice: Working with Corporate Culture and Organizational Change  **Guide:** *Corporate Culture and Organizational Change: Strategic Practice Guide* **Learning Organization Disciplines:** Shared Vision and System Thinking	Examine workplace situations from a cultural perspective in which the cultural stories told create patterns of actions. Examples include understanding why change interventions fail and how to make them succeed. As a result, you are able to conduct strategic practice experiences with others.
Systemic Storytelling and Emergent Leadership: Surfing the Waves of Change **Guide:** *Surfing the Waves of Change: Systemic Storytelling and Emergent Leadership Guide*  **Learning Organization Disciplines:** Personal Mastery, Mental Models, Shared Vision, Team Learning and System Thinking	Develop systemic eloquence by examining workplace situations using the decision support system trilogy of systems thinking, reflexive practice, and strategic practice, while applying the action learning approach. Examples include using these methods in real time while dealing with emerging issues, change, and opportunities. As a result, you are able to conduct decision support system experiences with others, thus creating the conditions for emergent leadership.
Organizational Design: Creating a Generative Learning Organization **Guide:** *Creating a Generative Learning Organization: Organizational Design Guide* **Learning Organization Disciplines:** Personal Mastery, Mental Models, Shared Team Learning and System Thinking	Develop an understanding of organizational energetics — how energy flows in terms of productivity, communication, learning, and creativity. Redesign and rethink governance, diffusion and strategies for creating generative learning organization.

Program Summary

The LTL Program is designed using the action learning process (see the yellow bar at the bottom of the diagram below). This means that you gain an understanding of your own patterns of thinking and acting in relation to the course concepts. You select a work-related action learning case, which you explore during each course. After each course, you take action on this work-related action learning case (see the action learning loops, found at the top of the diagram below, that connect each course). During the next course, you report your learnings from taking action on your work-related action learning case.

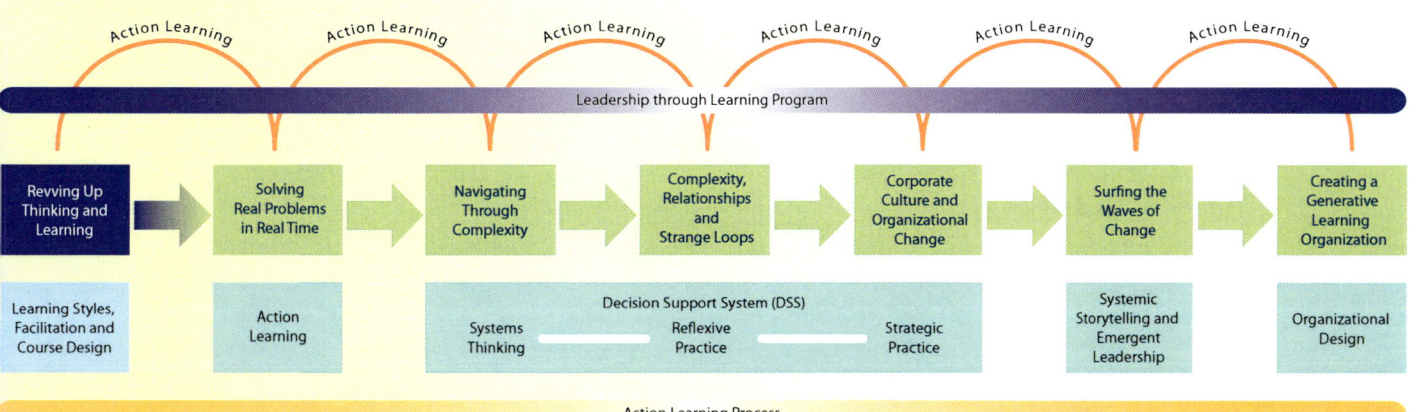

MHA Institute Certification

The LTL Program is designed using two key processes: action learning and a systemic approach. Action learning is about *learning as you go* by solving real problems in real time. *Learning as you go* is based on an experimental frame and is emergent in nature, lowering risk, and maximizing results. It is fundamental to building resilience in any system. A systemic approach is about approaching the future as a blank slate full of multiple possibilities, opening yourself to the possibility of creating something truly *novel*, sustainable and generative.

- **Leader/Team Certification**

The Leadership Through Learning (LTL) Program develops leaders and teams who learn at the speed of change and thrive in paradox, and who can mentor leadership and team development in others. Leaders and teams learn how to restart the wheel of learning that is resident in each person. Through the *Leadership Through Learning (LTL) Program*, leaders and teams learn how to create an environment that puts learning and the learner in the driver's seat.

- **Practitioner Certifcation**

The *Practitioner Development Program* develops practitioners who mentor leadership development in others, so that they can learn at the speed of change and thrive in paradox. Practitioners learn how to restart the wheel of learning that is resident in each person. Through the *Leadership Through Learning (LTL) Program*, practitioners learn how to create an environment that puts learning and the learner in the driver's seat.

Those wishing to qualify for an MHA Institute Certification must complete all requirements. For more information, go to the MHA website at www.mhainstitute.ca.

University Certification

The MHA Institute LTL Program is part of the Certificate for Continuing and Adult Education through the University of Alberta Faculty of Extension, Edmonton, Alberta, Canada. For more information, go to the MHA website at www.mhainstitute.ca.

Return on Investment

Early in the LTL Program, you identify specific return on investment objectives and measures for both yourself and your organization. The LTL Program requires you to take action in the workplace, both during and after each course, in order to create sustainable and measurable return on investment.

Public Courses

These courses are offered to the public through a number of institutions. For more information go to the MHA website at wwwmhainstituteca.

MHA INSTITUTE | mentoring human action

PO Box 4590, Edmonton AB T6E 2A0
P: 780.686.4128 F: 780.481.7956
E-mail: info@mhainstitute.ca Web: www.mhainstitute.ca
Blog: www.leadershipthroughlearning.ca

Learning Styles Questionnaire (LSQ)

Interpretation Guide

Leadership in Action Series

Version A

Marilyn Herasymowych & Henry Senko

MHA | mentoring
INSTITUTE | human
          | action

MHA Institute Inc. Publication
Edmonton, Alberta, Canada

This document is written by Marilyn Herasymowych and Henry Senko,
and edited by Joan Heys Hawkins.
Cover art and format of Guide designed by Joan Heys Hawkins.
Images used in this document are protected by copyright.
© 1999-2006 Ralph Hagen, *All Rights Reserved.*

Library and Archives Canada Cataloguing in Publication

Herasymowych, Marilyn, 1955-
       Learning styles questionnaire (LSQ) : interpretation guide / Marilyn
Herasymowych, Henry Senko ; edited by Joan Heys Hawkins ; images by Ralph Hagen.

       Includes bibliographical references and index.
       ISBN 978-0-9737697-1-5

       1. Cognitive learning. 2. Cognitive styles.
       I. Senko, Henry, 1952- II. Hawkins, Joan Heys III. MHA Institute IV. Title
       BF318.H47 2006   153.1'5   C2006-902807-9

For information, contact:
MHA Institute Inc.
PO Box 4590
Edmonton, Alberta, Canada T6E 2A0
Email: info@mhainstitute.ca
Web: www.mhainstitute.ca

Table of Contents

Section 3: More Information

The Learning Cycle

Learning through action and reflection

People learn because they need to solve everyday problems. They solve problems by displaying four basic behaviours. Each of these behaviours arises from a specific learning orientation. These four behaviours and their associated learning orientations are shown below in a diagram called the *Learning Cycle*.

Reference
The *Learning Cycle* and other variations of this cycle used in this Guide are based on the work of David Kolb and his *Experiential Learning Cycle*. It is also based on the work of a number of other researchers, including Peter Honey and Alan Mumford, Peter Senge, Bernice McCarthy, Reg Revans, Kristina Weinstein, and John C. Redding and Ralph F. Catalanello. For more information, see Section 3, *Research References*, page 49.

Learning Cycle

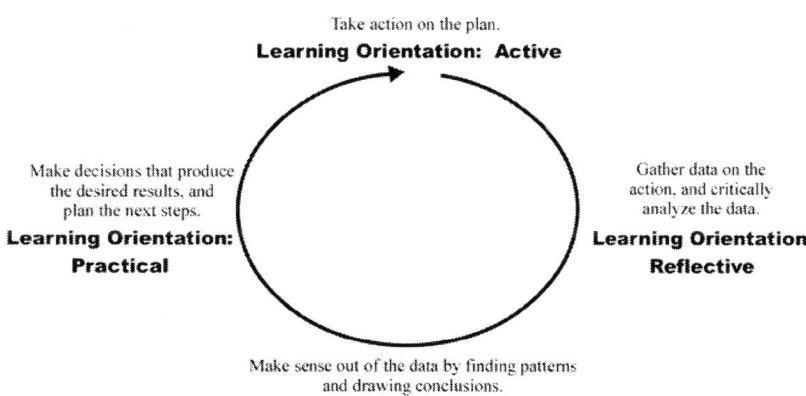

Each learning orientation in the *Learning Cycle* leads to the next, thus creating a circular dynamic. However, when operating, the cycle is actually a spiral that loops through taking action and reflecting on the action taken (shown below).

Spiral of Learning

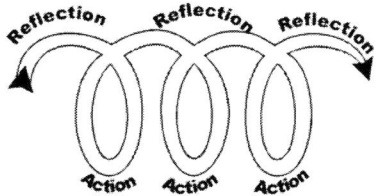

The spiral nature of learning means that, as we learn and create new knowledge, we also create new and novel ways of thinking, knowing, and learning. Thus, the cycle of learning is never the same. Like a great wheel, every rotation puts us in a different place, with new knowledge and new learning.

It is difficult to show this spiral nature of learning in a two-dimensional model, such as the *Learning Cycle* (shown below). To attempt to show this in the model, there is line dividing the *Learning Cycle* into two parts, and on either side of this line are the words *Action* and *Reflection*.

Learning Cycle: Action and Reflection

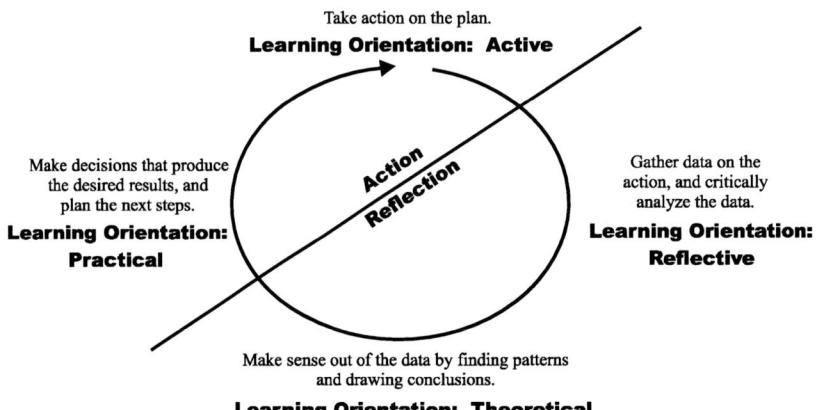

Take action on the plan.
Learning Orientation: Active

Make decisions that produce the desired results, and plan the next steps.
Learning Orientation: Practical

Action
Reflection

Gather data on the action, and critically analyze the data.
Learning Orientation: Reflective

Make sense out of the data by finding patterns and drawing conclusions.
Learning Orientation: Theoretical

This division is meant to illustrate the movement between action and reflection:

- **Reflection:** In this state, people spend time thinking, rather than acting. There are two learning orientations that are reflection-based in nature: *reflective* and *theoretical*.

- **Action:** In this state, people spend time acting, rather than thinking. There are two learning orientations that are action-based in nature: *practical* and *active*.

These two parts of the cycle, as well as the four learning orientations, are in a dynamic relationship with each other (i.e., the spiral of learning). To understand this dynamic, it helps to understand each of the four learning orientations in more depth.

Learning Orientations

Four learning orientations

Note

The authors have collected many of the descriptors on pages 6-9 from teams in organizations, and from participants in their courses on learning styles. These people, who have examined their learning style profiles in depth, have supplied and verified all of the descriptors shown on pages 6-9.

There are four learning orientations, and each one has specific characteristics that define it. Each person has a *learning style profile*, in which each of the four orientations is exhibited to some degree. In order to understand how a person's learning style profile might look, we need to understand each of the orientations in more detail. It is highly unlikely that any one person displays only one learning orientation as a style. However, this is how each orientation is explained in this Section — as if the other three orientations were not affecting the one being described.

Each learning orientation is described using the following areas:

- **Strengths:** The best of the orientation
- **Drawbacks:** The possible drawbacks of the orientation
- **Indicators:** The behaviours that indicate that this orientation is in play
- **Attitude:** Whether or not this orientation is an open or closed style
- **Types of questions this orientation asks:** General questions that someone operating from this orientation might ask
- **Thinking Style:** Types of thinking at which someone operating from this orientation might be good
- **What to give a person of this orientation as a gift:** A fun, personal way of looking at learning orientations

To be strong in any of the learning orientations, you do not have to display all of the characteristics listed. If you display 50% or more of the characteristics in an orientation, it is likely that you are strong in that orientation.

Reflective Learning Orientation

Strengths	• Highly tolerant of others • Good listener • Very polite
Drawbacks	• Has difficulty bringing closure • Often called *procrastinator* by other styles • Does not see himself or herself as a procrastinator; simply wants enough time to consider options and data
Indicators	• Collectors of information • Often have collections as hobbies
Attitudes	• Open to new ideas • Open to new data
Types of questions this orientation asks	People with a reflective orientation ask questions to obtain more data, such as: • What do we know? • What do we not know? • What do we need to know?
Thinking Style	• **Critical Analysis:** You are using critical analysis when you verify the accuracy and validity of data and evidence. • **Systems Thinking:** You are using systems thinking when you consider the parts of the system, and the system as a whole.
What to give a person of this orientation as a gift	• People with a strong reflective orientation want time to spend as they see fit. For example, they may want to spend all day in a hardware store. • If you know what a person with a reflective orientation collects, you can buy something for this collection.

Theoretical Learning Orientation

Strengths	<ul><li>Excellent synthesizer of disparate information</li><li>Articulate</li><li>Able to synthesize complex ideas into simple models</li></ul>
Drawbacks	<ul><li>Has difficulty being open to perspectives that are not grounded in theory</li><li>Often called *arrogant* by other styles</li><li>Does not see himself or herself as arrogant; simply wants everything to be backed up by proof</li></ul>
Indicators	<ul><li>Thinkers about theories</li><li>Often readers of non-fiction based in their field of expertise or interest</li></ul>
Attitudes	<ul><li>Sceptical of new ideas</li><li>Open to certain types of data</li></ul>
Types of questions this orientation asks	People with a theoretical orientation ask questions to make sense and draw conclusions, such as: <ul><li>Why do we need to do this?</li><li>How does this fit into the big picture?</li><li>What does this mean?</li></ul>
Thinking Style	<ul><li>**Systems Thinking:** You are using systems thinking when you consider the relationships among the parts of the system, and the system as a whole.</li><li>**Creative Thinking:** You are using creative thinking when you generate ideas, alternative perspectives, and/or scenarios.</li></ul>
What to give a person of this orientation as a gift	<ul><li>People with a theoretical orientation know what they like, and, even if you know them well, it is likely that you might give them something that they already have.</li><li>Give people with a theoretical orientation money or gift certificates, and let them buy their own gifts.</li></ul>

Practical Learning Orientation

Strengths	• Able to plan • Able to make decisions • Able to take action on the plan
Drawbacks	• Has difficulty being open to perspectives that are not relevant • Often called *opinionated* by other styles • Does not see himself or herself as opinionated; simply wants everything to be practical and to fit into the plan
Indicators	• Busy doing something • Outspoken
Attitudes	• Sceptical of anything that is not immediately relevant and useful • Action-oriented
Types of questions this orientation asks	People with a practical orientation ask questions to make decisions and to take action, such as: • What decision do we need to make? • What is the plan? • How do we take action?
Thinking Style	• **Creative Thinking:** You are using creative thinking when you generate alternative scenarios and/or ways to take action. • **Strategic Thinking:** You are using strategic thinking when you decide what to do and what not to do.
What to give a person of this orientation as a gift	People with a practical orientation like gifts that are practical and useful.

Active Learning Orientation

Strengths	• Has faith that everything will work out • Will try almost anything • Is a lot of fun to be around
Drawbacks	• Has problems slowing down, and taking time to think things through • Often called *impulsive* by other styles • Does not see himself or herself as a impulsive; simply wants to give things a try
Indicators	• Verbal, not afraid to talk, and first to volunteer • Centre of attention
Attitudes	• Open to new ideas • Will try anything once
Types of questions this orientation asks	People with an active orientation ask questions to take action, such as: • When do we start? • Why not? • What other ideas are out there?
Thinking Style	• **Action Thinking:** You are using action thinking when you are in the midst of action. • **Creative Thinking:** You are using creative thinking when you generate new ideas that may not have been thought of before.
What to give a person of this orientation as a gift	• People with an active orientation want to experience things, and they prefer company. Be prepared to share an experience with them. • People with an active orientation are usually happy with any gift, no matter how small.

Learning Style Profile

Profiling learning

Reference
The *Learning Styles Questionnaire* was developed by Peter Honey and Alan Mumford to help managers to understand how they learn and solve problems. You can complete the LSQ, and, through a process of validation, arrive at a learning style profile that illustrates how you learn, make decisions, and solve problems. To determine your learning style profile, see Section 2, *Your Learning Style Profile*, page 17.

A *learning style profile* shows you how the learning orientations work in combination with each other. You do not have to determine your learning style profile to understand this section. However, if you wish, you can do that before reading further. You can determine your learning style profile by completing the *Learning Styles Questionnaire* (LSQ). Instructions for completing the LSQ are found in Section 2 (see sidebar *Reference* for more information).

When people complete the LSQ, and validate their results, they get a visual picture of their learning style profile, which looks like the one shown below. The profile is often referred to as a *kite*, because of its shape.

Mark's Learning Style Profile

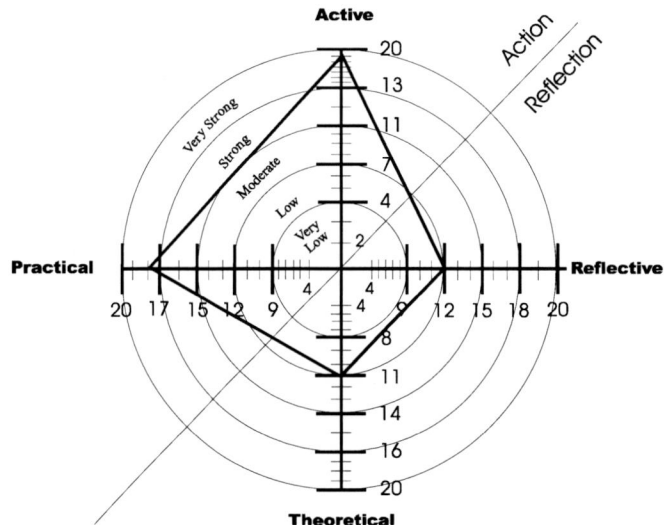

Interpreting the learning style profile

Once you know your profile, you can interpret it using the characteristics of the four learning orientations.

Interpreting Mark's Learning Style Profile

Using Mark's learning style profile from the previous page, one can say that Mark has a:

- **Low score in the reflective orientation:** This means that it is likely that Mark does not gather information readily. Instead, he is more likely to use the information at hand.

- **Low score in the theoretical orientation:** This means that it is likely that Mark does not spend much time considering his options, and drawing conclusions on what he has considered. It is more likely that Mark draws conclusions quickly, with little or no thought.

- **High score in the practical orientation:** This means that Mark is likely to want practical and relevant solutions, and decisions that result in action. He may want to plan how to implement an action.

- **High score in the active orientation:** This means that Mark is likely to be willing to take action quickly, having faith that it will work out. If it does not work out, Mark probably believes that he can figure it out as he goes.

Looking at the visual representation of Mark's profile, one can see that the greater area of his profile (shaded in grey) is above the diagonal line of *Action* and *Reflection*, showing Mark to be an action-based learner.

Mark's Learning Style Profile: Action-based

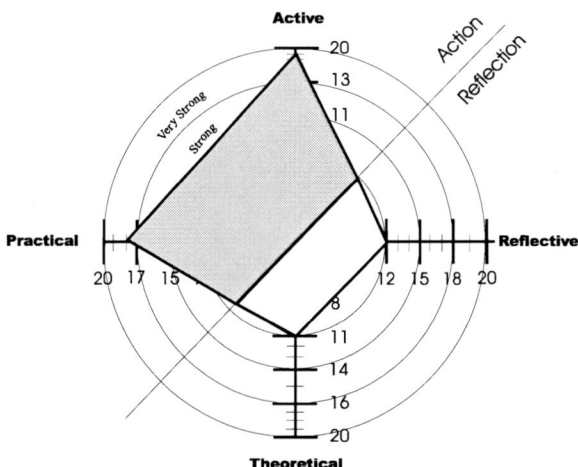

Mark's short cuts in the reflection-based learning orientations may cause him to believe that he has enough information, and has drawn the correct conclusions, when, in fact, he is likely to have paid little attention to these processes. To others, Mark is seen as a *doer*, someone who is quick to make decisions, to solve problems, and to take actions. Mark may be seen as impatient with the reflection process. The result is that Mark may inadvertently compromise his effectiveness in managing both people and work. In a classroom, he may be impatient for action, and vocalize his displeasure when there is too much theory being presented.

Note

There is a tendency to believe that we use only one learning orientation, when, in fact, we have the capacity to use all four, depending on the situation. However, even though we have access to all four learning orientations, we have preferences for some orientations over others. In their research, the authors have found that most people have two or three orientations that they use with confidence, and one or two non-preferences that they use with less confidence.

While the active learner sometimes jumps into things without forethought, the theoretical learner often spends just too much time reading.

Interpreting Mark's Learning Style Profile (continued)

Mark's learning style profile is a visual representation of his preferred way to learn. His low scores in the reflective and theoretical orientations are non-preferred. Although his profile kite shape looks skewed, it is, in fact, very effective much of the time. However, at those times when the situation calls for more reflection, Mark's profile, and resulting behaviours, are ineffective. For Mark to be able to deal with these novel situations, he needs to stretch himself beyond his preferred orientations into those that he finds more difficult and possibly boring.

Traditionally, many educators have believed that it is important for learners to learn while using only their preferred learning styles. The authors have found that people learn most deeply when they have a whole learning experience that causes them to experience all four orientations. One of the reasons this happens is because the wheel of learning engages us in another wheel — the wheel of thinking.

The Wheel of Thinking

Defining thinking

In this Guide, the authors define *thinking* as the broad area of cognition. Cognition comprises alertness, disposition, concentration, perceptual speed, learning, memory, problem solving, decision making, reasoning, sense making, and creativity. Cognition includes everything from how you pick up information, to how your brain sets down patterns, to how you make sense or meaning. In the end, what is crucial is how you respond to your world, as well as how you reshape it through your creativity and intelligence.

Expert thinkers

An expert thinker is someone who:

- Is skilled in a variety of thinking approaches (e.g., critical thinking, strategic thinking, creative thinking)
- Knows when to use the different thinking approaches
- Is disposed to think
- Makes whatever he or she is thinking about relevant to his or her situation

Expert thinkers think about their thinking (i.e., metacognition), which is a key skill in enhancing thinking capacity.

Reference
David Perkins has coined the term *expert learner*. The authors have expanded Perkins' term to encompass *expert thinking* as well.

Perkins is a senior research associate at the Harvard Graduate School of Education, and author of several books. For more information, see Section 3, *Research References*, page 49.

Types of thinking

Note
The authors have developed these five types of thinking based on the definitions on this page, and on their research in effective course design. Other researchers may define these types of thinking differently.

This Guide focuses on five different types of thinking that are directly connected to the four learning orientations (shown below).

Types of Thinking

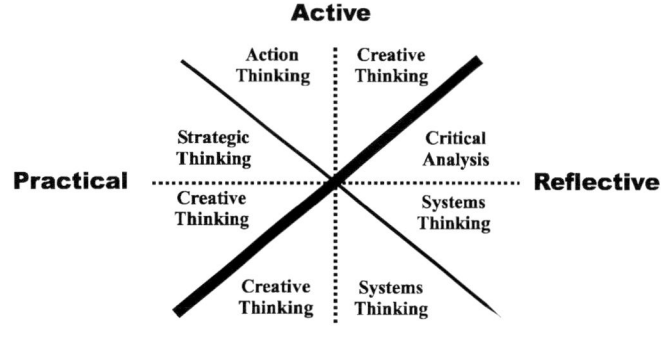

Critical analysis

Critical analysis verifies the accuracy and validity of data and evidence (*reflective* learning orientation).

Systems thinking

Systems thinking considers the system:

- *Reflective* learning orientation considers the parts of the system, and the system as a whole.

- *Theoretical* learning orientation considers the relationships among the parts of the system, and the system as a whole.

Creative thinking

Creative thinking generates alternatives:

- *Theoretical* learning orientation creates innovative ideas (e.g., records, audiotapes, and CDs are innovations of the invention of a record player).

- *Practical* learning orientation creates innovative ways to implement ideas.

- *Active* learning orientation creates inventive ideas.

Strategic thinking

Strategic thinking is about deciding what to do and what not to do (*practical* learning orientation).

Action thinking

Action thinking is used in the midst of action (*active* learning orientation).

15

Your Learning Style Profile

Instructions   The following section and set of instructions are meant to be used with the following two booklets (found at the back of this Guide:

- *Learning Styles Questionnaire* (referred to as the *Blue Booklet*)
- *Capitalizing on Your Learning Style* (referred to as the *Beige Booklet*)

Learning Styles Questionnaire (LSQ)   You will use the *Blue Booklet*, along with these instructions, to:

1. Complete the questionnaire.
2. Score the questionnaire.
3. Graph your LSQ profile on the *Normed Graph* on page 26 of this Guide.
4. Complete the first validation activity to validate your LSQ profile.

Capitalizing on Your Learning Style   You will use the *Beige Booklet*, along with these instructions to:

5. Complete the second validation activity to further validate your LSQ profile.
6. Identify excuses that you use to short cut certain learning orientations.
7. Identify ways to improve strength in your learning orientations.

Interpretation instructions   Once you have completed the instructions above, and determined your learning style profile, you can continue to:

8. Complete other activities to understand your LSQ profile in more depth.

Completing the LSQ

For these instructions, you will need:

- The *Blue Booklet*

- The *Normed Graph* found on page 26 (you may want to photocopy page 26)

1. Read the first page of the *Blue Booklet*.

2. In the *Blue Booklet*, notice that the inventory is on pages 2-4 and that the *Response Sheet* is on page 5. Remove the *Response Sheet*, so that it will be easier for you to record your responses.

3. Complete the inventory by thinking of how you operate in a working situation more often than not. Make sure that you respond to the statements as honestly as possible. On the *Response Sheet*:

   a. Circle the letter **A** for *agree* if the statement describes what you are like at work.

   b. Circle the letter **D** for *disagree* if the statement describes what you are not like at work.

Note

This questionnaire works best if you have a response for each of the statements. However, some people do struggle with responding to some of the statements. If you are struggling with making a choice, try one or more of the approaches below. You will validate the results of this questionnaire later:

- Respond to how you would act 51% or more of the time.

- Complete as much of the questionnaire as you can, then go back to respond to the statements that you skipped.

- Flip a coin.

- If you are still unsure about the statement and/or have questions about the statement, circle D for disagree.

To derive more in-depth information about yourself from the LSQ, complete the following instructions:

4. Make a note of any statements of which you are unsure. Beside each of these statements, record the reason for your uncertainty. Here are some possible reasons:

    a. Your response depends on the situation.

    Note

    If you have selected this reason, it may be that you are caught between two learning styles.

    b. You do not want to admit that you behave in the way that the statement is suggesting.

    Note

    If you have selected this reason, this may help you to decide which characteristics you wish to modify, in order to become more effective.

    c. You wish you did behave in the way the statement is suggesting.

    Note

    If you have selected this reason, this may help you to decide which characteristics you wish to develop, in order to be more effective.

5. Even though the LSQ is not timed, note how long it takes you to complete it. Below is a possible interpretation of what this information may mean in terms of your learning style profile:

   • If you take more than 20 minutes to complete the LSQ, it is likely that you are more reflection-based.

   • If you take less than 20 minutes to complete the LSQ, it is likely that you are more action-based.

Scoring the LSQ

Note
Honey and Mumford use the term *learning styles*; this Guide uses *learning orientations*.

Once you have completed the LSQ:

1. Separate the 2 pages of the *Response Sheet*. The second sheet is called the *Scoring Sheet*.

2. Read the instructions at the top of the *Scoring Sheet*. When you have completed scoring, you will have 4 totals at the bottom of the page, one for each of the 4 learning styles (orientations):

   • Activist (same as the active learning orientation)

   • Reflector (same as the reflective learning orientation)

   • Theorist (same as the theoretical learning orientation)

   • Pragmatist (same as the practical learning orientation)

3. This is your *raw score*. Graph each of these numbers on the appropriate axis on the *Normed Graph* on page 26. In the legend on the *Normed Graph*, beside the words *Raw Score*, record the colour of pen you used to draw your learning styles profile.

4. Join the 4 points on the graph, so that they look like a kite. On the next page is an example of a graphed kite.

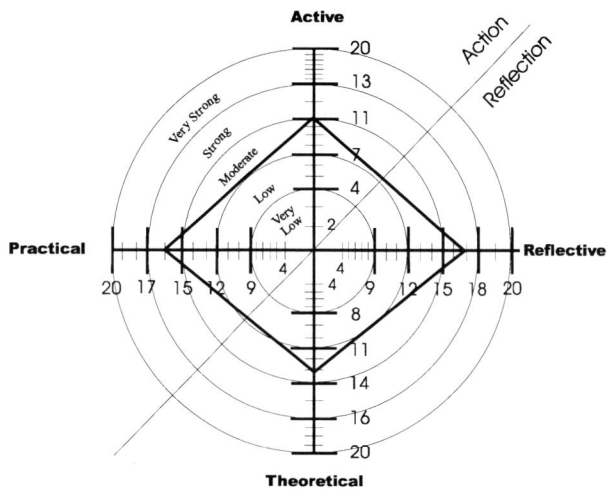

Validating your LSQ results

In the authors' experience of using the LSQ with people in a number of different situations, they have discovered that many people do not get a valid learning style profile simply from completing the questionnaire. This is why they developed the following 3 validation activities, so that you can diagram a valid learning style profile.

Each time you do a validation activity, you will be asked to look at the current profile diagrammed on the *Normed Graph* (page 26), and decide whether or not you want to change the profile, and, if so, how you will make the changes.

At the end of the 3 validation activities, you will determine your actual learning style profile. When you have done this, you can diagram that profile in this *Guide* (page 26).

First validation

To complete the first validation:

1. Read the descriptions for each learning orientation listed on pages 7-8 of the *Blue Booklet*. Highlight the sentences that best describe you. If you cannot highlight the entire sentence, highlight as much of the sentence that applies to you.

2. View your highlighting to gain a visual perspective. Visually, you may see that some of the learning orientations have more highlighting than others. The more highlighting in a learning orientation, the stronger your preference is for that learning orientation.

3. Notice that the *Normed Graph* (page 26) has 5 circles, and that each circle is labelled as follows (see the diagram below):

   - **Very Low:** This means that you have very little or no strength in this learning orientation.

   - **Low:** This means that you have little strength in this learning style.

   - **Moderate:** This means that you have moderate strength in this learning orientation.

   - **Strong:** This means that you have a fair amount of strength in this learning orientation.

   - **Very Strong:** This means that you have considerable strength in this learning orientation.

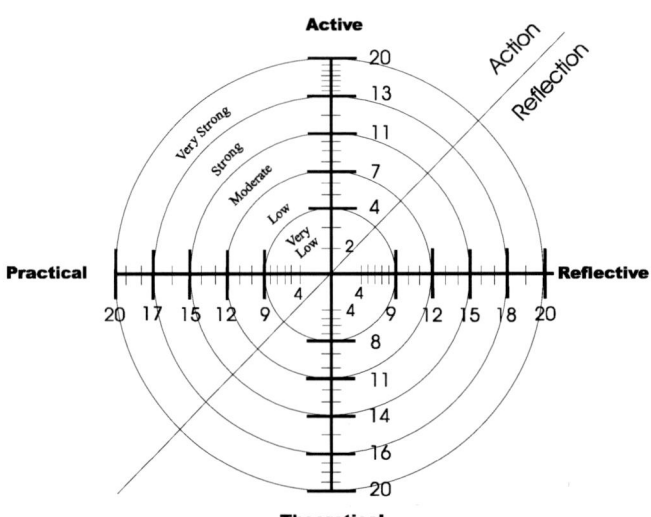

4. Compare your raw score on the *Normed Graph* (page 26) to see how the scores match what you have highlighted in the learning orientations on pages 7-8 in the *Blue Book*let.

5. View your highlighting of the learning orientations again. Remember, the more highlighting, the stronger your preference for that learning orientation. Use the following guidelines to help you in your choices:

- If you highlighted less than 20% of the description, it is likely that you have a *very low* to *low* score in this learning orientation.

- If you highlighted about half of the description, it is likely that you have a *moderate* score in this learning orientation.

- If you highlighted more than 70% of the description, it is likely that you have a *strong* to *very strong* score in this learning orientation.

- If you highlighted all of the description, it is likely that you have a *very strong* score in this learning orientation.

- If your highlighting is too sparse for drawing any conclusions, make no changes and go on to the next validation.

6. Make any changes to your learning styles profile that you feel are valid. Use a different colour to show any changes you have made on the *Normed Graph* (page 26), and record that colour in the legend beside the words *First Validation*.

Second validation

To complete the second validation:

1. Notice that each learning style is described in more detail on pages 8-11 of the *Beige Booklet*. Notice that each description has 2 parts:

- *... you will learn **best** from activities where:*

- *... you will learn **least** from activities where:*

Note
The second part of the learning style description tells you more about your learning orientation than the first part of the description. The reason is that, as learners, people always know when they are uncomfortable in a learning situation.

2. First, read the top half of each description (*... you will learn **best** from activities where:*). Highlight the statements that best describe how you learn **best**. If you cannot highlight the entire sentence, highlight as much as you can.

3. Second, read the bottom half of each description (*... you will learn **least** from activities where:*). Highlight the sentences that best describe how you *do not* learn. If you cannot highlight the entire sentence, highlight as much as you can.

4. View your highlighting to gain a visual perspective. Visually, you may see that some of the learning orientations have more highlighting than others. The more highlighting, the stronger your preference for that learning orientation. Use the following guidelines to help you in your choices:

   - If you highlighted less than 20% of the entire description, it is likely that you have a *very low* to *low* score in this learning orientation.

   - If you highlighted about half of the entire description, it is likely that you have a *moderate* score in this learning orientation.

   - If you highlighted more than 70% of the entire description, it is likely that you have a *strong* to *very strong* score in this learning orientation.

   - If you highlighted all of the description, it is likely that you have a *very strong* score in this learning orientation.

   - Regardless of how much highlighting you may have in the first part of the description, if you highlighted all, or almost all, of the second part of the description, you have a *strong* score in this learning orientation.

5. Make any changes to your learning style profile that you feel are valid. Use a different colour to show any changes you have made on the *Normed Graph* (page 26), and record that colour in the legend beside the words *Second Validation*.

Third validation

To complete the third validation:

1. Read the information in Section 1, pages 6-9, which describes the four learning orientations. Highlight the descriptors that best describe you. Recall that this Guide has different names for the learning orientations indicated in the LSQ:

    - Activist (same as the active learning orientation)

    - Reflector (same as the reflective learning orientation)

    - Theorist (same as the theoretical learning orientation)

    - Pragmatist (same as the practical learning orientation)

2. View your highlighting, and decide if you are *very low*, *low*, *moderate*, *strong*, or *very strong* in that orientation.

3. Make any changes to your learning style profile that you feel are valid. Use a different colour to show any changes you have made on the *Normed Graph* on the next page, and record that colour in the legend beside the words *Third Validation*.

LSQ Activity 1:
Learning style
profile

Below is your validated learning style profile.

Normed Graph

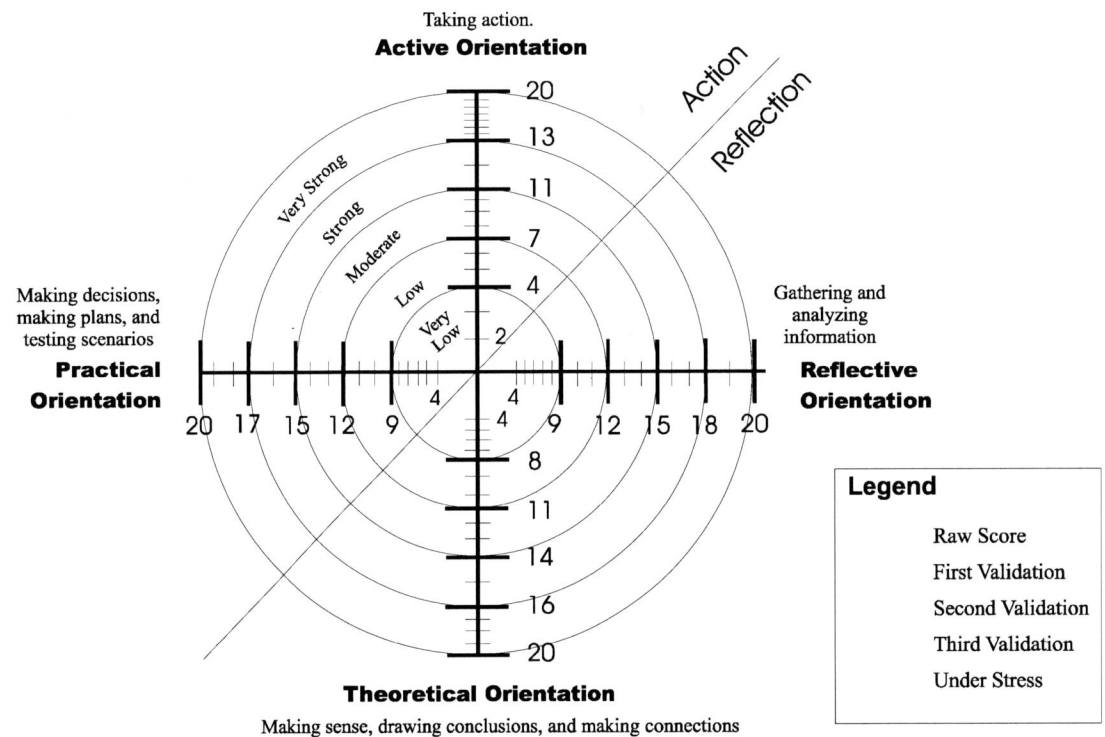

Taking action.
Active Orientation

Making decisions,
making plans, and
testing scenarios
Practical
Orientation

Gathering and
analyzing
information
Reflective
Orientation

Theoretical Orientation
Making sense, drawing conclusions, and making connections

Legend

Raw Score
First Validation
Second Validation
Third Validation
Under Stress

For now, do not pay attention to the table below. Go to the next page to continue. You may complete this table later.

Strengths	Weaknesses
Action to be taken	**Excuses for short cutting LSQ action item**

**LSQ Activity 2:
LSQ profile
interpretation**

Note

Since 1996, the authors have used the LSQ, and interpreted learning style profiles, with many people in many organizations. As a result of their work, and the data they have gathered, they have written this section. The authors wish to state that these descriptions are simplifications of a very complex learning style dynamic that people demonstrate. These descriptions are meant to be helpful in understanding different profiles, and are not meant to tell people how they should behave.

1. To recall the *Learning Cycle*, the four learning orientations, and how to interpret the learning style profile, review the information in Section 1, pages 1-13.

2. Recall your *validated learning style profile* on the *Normed Graph* on page 26. On the next few pages, there are several variations of the learning style profiles described. Each profile shape is described as it might manifest itself in the real world.

3. Review these profiles to find the one that is closest to your profile shape. Read the profile description, and highlight the descriptors that fit your behaviour the best. If you find more than one profile that seem to fit your profile shape, then read these profiles as well, and highlight the descriptors that fit your behaviour the best.

The profiles are listed in the following order:
- **Double-dominant profiles:**
  Profiles with strength in two learning orientations
- **Triple-dominant profiles:**
  Profiles with strength in three learning orientations
- **Quadruple-dominant profiles:**
  Profiles with strength in four learning orientations

There are no descriptions for single-dominant profiles, because the authors have not experienced anyone who displays strength in only one learning orientation. However, if you wish to know the descriptions for single-dominant profiles, see Section 1, pages 6-9.

Double-Dominant Profiles

Profile Shape	Profile Description
Learning Style Profile 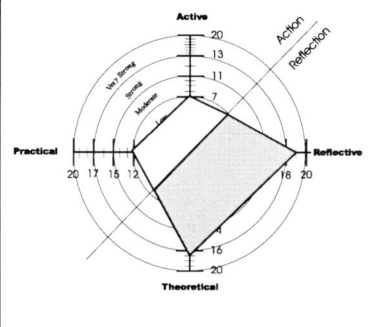	• **Strong/Very Strong score in the reflective orientation:** This means that you probably gather information readily. You are likely to be open to all sorts of information and ideas. You may find that deadlines increase pressure on you. • **Strong/Very Strong score in the theoretical orientation:** This means that that you probably spend much time considering your options, and drawing conclusions on what you have considered. Even though you draw conclusions, it is likely that the strong/very strong score in reflective orientation can cause a *wobble* between your desire for closure and your desire to remain open. • **Low/Moderate score in the practical orientation:** This means that you are unlikely to be concerned with practical and relevant solutions, and decisions that result in action. You may struggle with making decisions, although a moderate score may make it easier for you to make decisions, and to plan how to implement an action. • **Low/Moderate score in the active orientation:** This means that you are unlikely to be willing to take action quickly, and to have faith that it will work out. Even with a moderate score in this orientation, it is likely that you are risk-averse. In the reflection-based visual representation of this profile, the greater area of this profile (shaded in grey) is below the diagonal line of *Action* and *Reflection*, showing it to be a reflection-based learning style.

Profile Short Cuts	Opportunity for Learning
This profile's short cuts in the action-based learning orientations may cause you to believe that you cannot make decisions to take action without enough information and thought. To others, you might be seen as a *thinker*, someone who is thoughtful and considers many points of view. You may be seen as procrastinating. The result is that you may inadvertently compromise your effectiveness in managing both people and work. In a classroom, you may be overly quiet and reflective, and feel uncomfortable when asked to speak in a large group or participate in an activity.	This learning style profile is a visual representation of a preferred way to learn. The low scores in the practical and active orientations are non-preferred. Although this profile kite shape looks skewed, it is, in fact, very effective much of the time. However, at those times when the situation calls for more action, this profile, and its resulting behaviours, are ineffective. For you to be able to deal with these novel situations, you need to stretch yourself beyond these preferred orientations into those that you find more difficult, and possibly anxiety provoking.

Profile Shape	Profile Description
Learning Style Profile 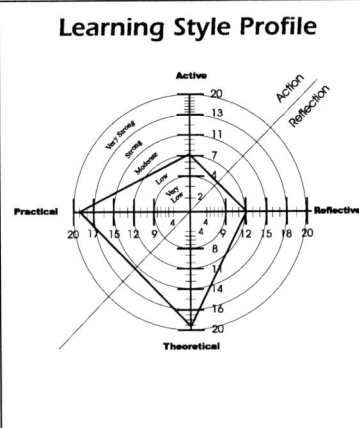 **Reflection/Action-Based Profile** 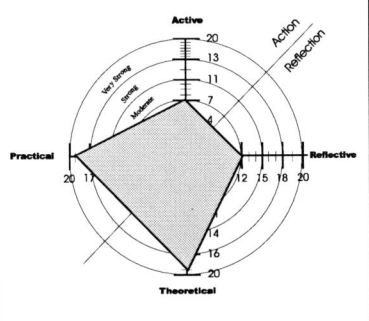	• **Low/Moderate score in the reflective orientation:** This means that you probably do not gather information readily. Instead, you are more likely to use the information at hand. If your score is moderate, you may search for information. • **Strong/Very Strong score in the theoretical orientation:** This means that you might easily consider your options, and draw conclusions. Once you draw conclusions, it is likely that you have difficulty changing your mind. This closed stance can be reinforced by a strong/very strong score in practical orientation. • **Strong/Very Strong score in the practical orientation:** This means that you are likely to want practical and relevant decisions, solutions, and plans that result in action. Innovative thinking and action occur when there is strength in both the theoretical and practical orientations. You may be very good at generating ideas. • **Low/Moderate score in the active orientation:** This means that you are unlikely to take action that is based on intuition. Even with a moderate score in this orientation, it is likely that you are risk-averse to actions that do not make practical sense to you. In the reflection/action-based visual representation of this profile, the area of this profile (shaded in grey) is on both sides of the diagonal line of *Action* and *Reflection*, showing it to be a both a reflection- and an action-based learning style.

Profile Short Cuts	Opportunity for Learning
The short cut in the reflective learning orientation may cause you to believe that you have enough information to draw a conclusion. The short cut in the active learning orientation may cause you to believe that your decision to take only practical action is good enough. As a result, you may be seen as arrogant, rigid, and closed, because you believe that you are right. The result is that you may inadvertently compromise your effectiveness in managing both people and work. To others, you might be seen as someone who gets the job done. In a classroom, you may be overly critical and impatient, and feel uncomfortable when there is too much theory, or activities that seem irrelevant.	This learning style profile is a visual representation of a preferred way to learn. The low scores in the reflective and active orientations are non-preferred. Although this profile kite shape looks skewed, it is, in fact, very effective much of the time. However, at those times when the situation calls for more openness, this profile, and its resulting behaviours, are ineffective. For you to be able to deal with these novel situations, you need to stretch yourself beyond these preferred orientations into those that you find more difficult, boring, and irrelevant.

Profile Shape	Profile Description
Learning Style Profile 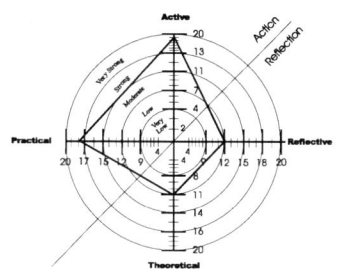 **Action-Based Profile** 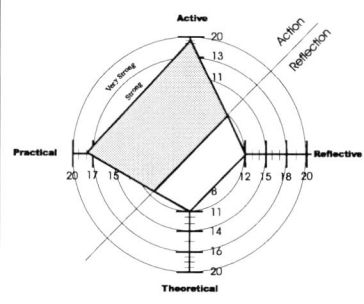	• **Low/Moderate score in the reflective orientation:** This means that you probably do not gather information readily. Instead, you are more likely to use the information at hand. If your score is moderate, you may search for information. • **Low/Moderate score in the theoretical orientation:** This means that you probably do not spend much time considering your options, and drawing conclusions on what you have considered. It is more likely that you draw conclusions quickly, with moderate, little, or no thought. • **Strong/Very Strong score in the practical orientation:** This means that you probably want practical and relevant solutions, and decisions that result in action. You may want to plan how to implement an action. • **Strong/Very Strong score in the active orientation:** This means that you are probably willing to take action quickly, having faith that it will work out. If it does not work out, you probably believe that you can figure it out as you go. In the action-based visual representation of this profile, the greater area of this profile (shaded in grey) is above the diagonal line of *Action* and *Reflection*, showing it to be an action-based learning style.
Profile Short Cuts	**Opportunity for Learning**
This profile's short cuts in the reflection-based learning orientations may cause you to believe that you have enough information, and have drawn the correct conclusions, when, in fact, you are likely to have paid little attention to these processes. To others, you might be seen as a *doer*, someone who is quick to make decisions, to solve problems, and to take actions. You may be seen as impatient with the reflection process. The result is that you may inadvertently compromise your effectiveness in managing both people and work. In a classroom, you may be impatient for action, and vocalize your displeasure when there is too much theory being presented.	This learning style profile is a visual representation of a preferred way to learn. The low scores in the reflective and theoretical orientations are non-preferred. Although this profile kite shape looks skewed, it is, in fact, very effective much of the time. However, at those times when the situation calls for more reflection, this profile, and its resulting behaviours, are ineffective. For you to be able to deal with these novel situations, you need to stretch yourself beyond these preferred orientations into those that you find more difficult, and possibly boring.

Profile Shape	Profile Description
Learning Style Profile 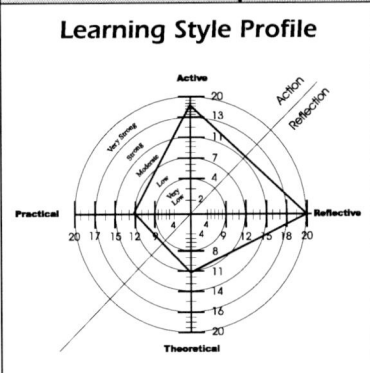 **Reflection/Action-Based Profile** 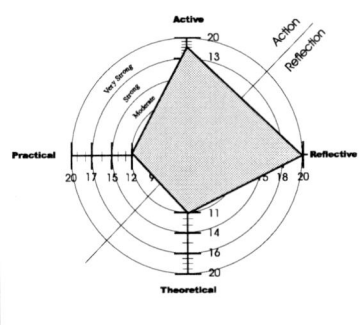	• **Strong/Very Strong score in the reflective orientation:** This means that you probably gather information readily. You are likely to be open to all sorts of information and ideas. You may find that deadlines increase pressure on you. • **Low/Moderate score in the theoretical orientation:** This means that you probably do not spend much time considering your options, and drawing conclusions on what you have considered. It is more likely that you draw conclusions quickly, with moderate, little, or no thought. • **Low/Moderate score in the practical orientation:** This means that you are unlikely to be concerned with practical and relevant solutions, and decisions that result in action. You may struggle with making decisions, although a moderate score may make it easier for you to make decisions, and to plan how to implement an action. • **Strong/Very Strong score in the active orientation:** This means that you are probably willing to take action quickly, having faith that it will work out. If it does not work out, you probably believe that you can figure it out as you go. Coupled with the strong/very strong score in the reflective orientation, it is likely that you are highly creative, inventive, and intuitive, a direct result of strength in two open learning orientations. In the reflection/action-based visual representation of this profile, the area of this profile (shaded in grey) is on both sides of the diagonal line of *Action* and *Reflection*, showing it to be both a reflection- and an action-based learning style.

Profile Short Cuts	Opportunity for Learning
The short cuts in the theoretical learning orientation may cause you to be confused about your actions at times, because it can be difficult for you to explain why you act the way you do. To others, you might be seen as both a *thinker* and a *doer*, at times a contradiction. You may be seen as impulsive, too open, and not grounded in reality at times. The result is that you may inadvertently compromise your effectiveness in managing both people and work. In a classroom, you may be impatient when there is too much structure, and not enough time for a play of ideas.	This learning style profile is a visual representation of a preferred way to learn. The low scores in the theoretical and practical orientations are non-preferred. Although this profile kite shape looks skewed, it is, in fact, very effective much of the time. However, at those times when the situation calls for more closure, this profile, and its resulting behaviours, are ineffective. For you to be able to deal with these novel situations, you need to stretch yourself beyond these preferred orientations into those that you find more difficult, and possibly boring and tedious.

Profile Shape	Profile Description
Learning Style Profile 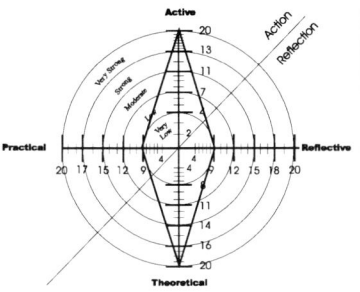 **Reflection/Action-Based Profile** 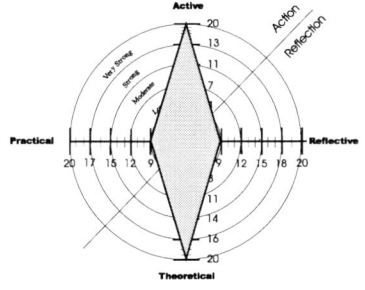	• **Low/Moderate score in the reflective orientation:** This means that it is likely that you do not gather information readily. Instead, you are more likely to use the information at hand. If your score is moderate, you may search for information. • **Strong/Very Strong score in the theoretical orientation:** This means that you might easily consider your options, and draw conclusions. Once you draw conclusions, it is likely that you have difficulty changing your mind. You are likely to have a strong desire to make sense of your experience. • **Low/Moderate score in the practical orientation:** This means that you are unlikely to be concerned with practical and relevant solutions, and decisions that result in action. You may struggle with making decisions, although a moderate score may make it easier for you to make decisions, and to plan how to implement an action. • **Strong/Very Strong score in the active orientation:** This means that you are probably willing to take action quickly, having faith that it will work out. If it does not work out, you probably believe that you can figure it out as you go. Coupled with strength in a theoretical orientation, you can come across as both closed and open at the same time, a seeming contradiction. In the reflection/action-based visual representation of this profile, the area of this profile (shaded in grey) is on both sides of the diagonal line of *Action* and *Reflection*, showing it to be both a reflection- and an action-based learning style.

Profile Short Cuts	Opportunity for Learning
The short cut in the reflective learning orientation may cause you to believe that you have enough information to draw conclusions. The short cut in the practical orientation may cause you to act impulsively. To others, you might be seen as a *doer*, someone who is quick to take actions. You may be seen as impatient with reflection and decision making processes. The result is that you may inadvertently compromise your effectiveness in managing both people and work. In a classroom, you may be impatient for action, and vocalize your displeasure when there is too much reflection.	This learning style profile is a visual representation of a preferred way to learn. The low scores in the reflective and practical orientations are non-preferred. Although this profile kite shape looks skewed, it is, in fact, very effective much of the time. However, at those times when the situation calls for more reflection, and planning, this profile, and its resulting behaviours, are ineffective. For you to be able to deal with these novel situations, you need to stretch yourself beyond these preferred orientations into those that you find more difficult, and possibly boring and irritating.

Profile Shape	Profile Description
Learning Style Profile 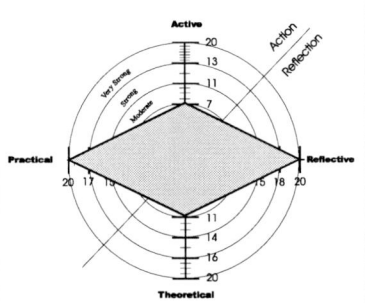 **Reflection/Action-Based Profile**	• **Strong/Very Strong score in the reflective orientation:** This means that you probably gather information readily. You are likely to be open to all sorts of information and ideas. You may find that deadlines increase pressure on you. • **Low/Moderate score in the theoretical orientation:** This means that you probably do not spend much time considering your options, and drawing conclusions on what you have considered. It is more likely that you draw conclusions quickly, with moderate, little, or no thought. • **Strong/Very Strong score in the practical orientation:** This means that you are likely to want practical and relevant solutions, and decisions that result in action. You may want to plan how to implement an action. • **Low/Moderate score in the active orientation:** This means that you are unlikely to take action that is based on intuition. Even with a moderate score in this orientation, it is likely that you are risk-averse to actions that do not make practical sense to you. In the reflection/action-based visual representation of this profile, the area of this profile (shaded in grey) is on both sides of the diagonal line of *Action* and *Reflection*, showing it to be both a reflection- and an action-based learning style.

Profile Short Cuts	Opportunity for Learning
The short cut in the theoretical learning orientation, and resulting confusion, may cause you to believe that you need to spend more time gathering information. The short cut in the active learning orientation may cause you to worry about whether or not to take action on what you perceive as risky ventures. To others, you might be seen as a *doer*, someone who is able to make decisions, to solve problems, and to take actions. You may be seen as risk averse. The result is that you may inadvertently compromise your effectiveness in managing both people and work. In a classroom, you are may be too impatient when there is a lack of relevance, or too much theory being presented.	This learning style profile is a visual representation of a preferred way to learn. The low scores in the theoretical and active orientations are non-preferred. Although this profile kite shape looks skewed, it is, in fact, very effective much of the time. However, at those times when the situation calls for more definite conclusions and intuitive actions, this profile, and its resulting behaviours, are ineffective. For you to be able to deal with these novel situations, you need to stretch yourself beyond these preferred orientations into those that you find more difficult, and possibly boring.

Triple-Dominant Profiles

Profile Shape	Profile Description
Learning Style Profile 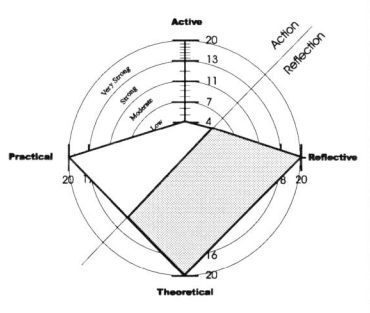 **Reflection-Based Profile**	• **Strong/Very Strong score in the reflective orientation:** This means that you probably gather information readily. You are likely to be open to all sorts of information and ideas. You may find that deadlines increase pressure on you. • **Strong/Very Strong score in the theoretical orientation:** This means that you probably spend time considering your options, and drawing conclusions. Once you draw conclusions, it is likely that you have difficulty changing your mind. Even though you draw conclusions, the strong/very strong score in reflective orientation can cause a *wobble* between your desire for closure and your desire to remain open. • **Strong/Very Strong score in the practical orientation:** This means that you are likely to want practical and relevant solutions, and decisions that result in action. You may want to plan how to implement an action. Even though you make decisions, the strong/very strong score in reflective orientation can cause a *wobble* back to the need to gather more information. • **Low/Moderate score in the active orientation:** This means that you are unlikely to take action that is based on intuition. Even with a moderate score in this orientation, it is likely that you are risk-averse to actions that do not make practical sense to you. In the reflection-based visual representation of this profile, the greater area of this profile (shaded in grey) is below the diagonal line of *Action* and *Reflection*, showing it to be a reflection-based learning style.
Profile Short Cuts	**Opportunity for Learning**
The short cut in the active learning orientation may cause you to worry about any action you might take, even actions that are practical in nature. To others, you might be seen as a *thinker*, someone who has to gather lots of data, mull over the data, and finds it difficult to make a decision. You may be seen as impatient with the reflection process. The result is that you may inadvertently compromise your effectiveness in managing both people and work. In a classroom, you may never be satisfied, seeming to want perfection.	This learning style profile is a visual representation of a preferred way to learn. The low score in the active orientation is non-preferred. Although this profile kite shape looks skewed, it is, in fact, very effective much of the time. However, at those times when the situation calls for more action, this profile, and its resulting behaviours, are ineffective. For you to be able to deal with these novel situations, you need to stretch yourself beyond these preferred orientations into the one that you find more difficult and anxiety provoking.

35

Profile Shape	Profile Description
Learning Style Profile 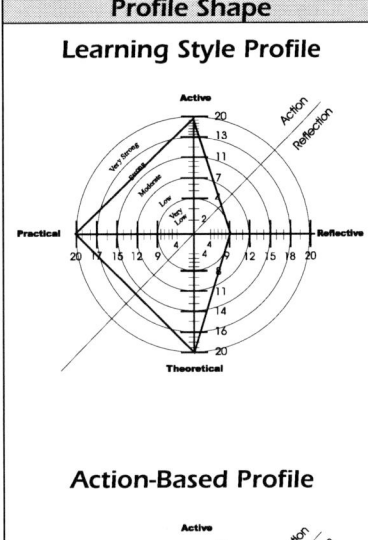 **Action-Based Profile**	• **Low/Moderate score in the reflective orientation:** This means that it is likely that you do not gather information readily. Instead, you are more likely to use the information at hand. If your score is moderate, you may search for information. • **Strong/Very Strong score in the theoretical orientation:** This means that you might easily consider your options, and draw conclusions. Once you draw conclusions, it is likely that you have difficulty changing your mind. • **Strong/Very Strong score in the practical orientation:** This means that you probably want practical and relevant solutions, and decisions that result in action. You may want to plan how to implement an action. • **Strong/Very Strong score in the active orientation:** This means that you are probably willing to take action quickly, having faith that it will work out. If it does not work out, you probably believe that you can figure it out as you go. In the action-based visual representation of this profile, the greater area of this profile (shaded in grey) is above the diagonal line of *Action* and *Reflection*, showing it to be an action-based learning style.

Profile Short Cuts	Opportunity for Learning
The short cut in the reflective learning orientation may cause you to believe that you have enough information. To others, you might be seen as a *doer*, someone who is articulate, able to make decisions, to solve problems, and to take actions. You may be seen as impatient with the reflection process. The result is that you may inadvertently compromise your effectiveness in managing both people and work. In a classroom, you may be impatient for action, and vocalize your displeasure when there is too much time being spent on reflection.	This learning style profile is a visual representation of a preferred way to learn. The low score in the reflective orientation is non-preferred. Although this profile kite shape looks skewed, it is, in fact, very effective much of the time. However, at those times when the situation calls for more information, this profile, and its resulting behaviours, are ineffective. For you to be able to deal with these novel situations, you need to stretch yourself beyond these preferred orientations into the one that you find more difficult, and possibly boring and tedious.

Profile Shape	Profile Description
Learning Style Profile 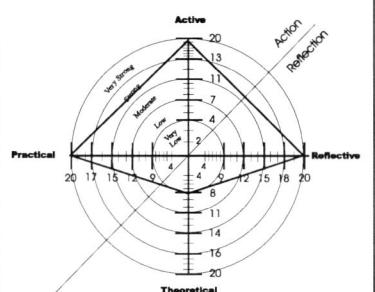 **Action-Based Profile** 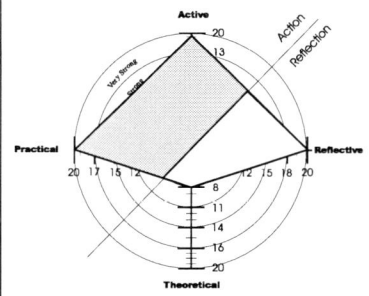	• **Strong/Very Strong score in the reflective orientation:** This means that you probably gather information readily. You are likely to be open to all sorts of information and ideas. • **Low/Moderate score in the theoretical orientation:** This means that you probably do not spend much time considering your options, and drawing conclusions on what you have considered. It is more likely that you draw conclusions quickly, with moderate, little, or no thought. • **Strong/Very Strong score in the practical orientation:** This means that you are likely to want practical and relevant solutions, and decisions that result in action. You may want to plan how to implement an action. • **Strong/Very Strong score in the active orientation:** This means that you are probably willing to take action quickly, having faith that it will work out. If it does not work out, you probably believe that you can figure it out as you go. In the action-based visual representation of this profile, the greater area of this profile (shaded in grey) is above the diagonal line of *Action* and *Reflection*, showing it to be an action-based learning style.

Profile Short Cuts	Opportunity for Learning
The short cut in the theoretical learning orientation may cause you to pay little or no attention to why a situation is the way it is, and making sense of the resulting confusion that situations bring. To others, you might be seen as a *doer*, someone who is reflective at times, but mostly able to make decisions, to solve problems, and to take actions. You may be seen as impatient with time spent trying to understand a situation and its context. The result is that you may inadvertently compromise your effectiveness in managing both people and work. In a classroom, you may be impatient for action, and vocalize your displeasure when there is too much theory being presented.	This learning style profile is a visual representation of a preferred way to learn. The low score in the theoretical orientation is non-preferred. Although this profile kite shape looks skewed, it is, in fact, very effective much of the time. However, at those times when the situation calls for more sense making, this profile, and its resulting behaviours, are ineffective. For you to be able to deal with these novel situations, you need to stretch yourself beyond these preferred orientations into the one that you find more difficult, and possibly confusing.

Profile Shape	Profile Description
Learning Style Profile 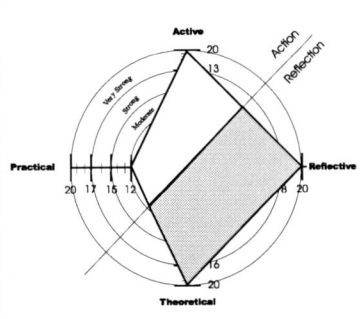 **Reflection-Based Profile**	• **Strong/Very Strong score in the reflective orientation:** This means that you probably gather information readily. You are likely to be open to all sorts of information and ideas. You may find that deadlines increase pressure on you. • **Strong/Very Strong score in the theoretical orientation:** This means that you probably spend much time considering your options, and drawing conclusions on what you have considered. Even though you draw conclusions, the strong/very strong score in reflective orientation can cause a *wobble* between your desire for closure and your desire to remain open. • **Low/Moderate score in the practical orientation:** This means that you are unlikely to be concerned with practical and relevant solutions, and decisions that result in action. You may struggle with making decisions, although a moderate score may make it easier for you to make decisions, and to plan how to implement an action. • **Strong/Very Strong score in the active orientation:** This means that you are probably willing to take action quickly, having faith that it will work out. If it does not work out, you probably believe that you can figure it out as you go. In the reflection-based visual representation of this profile, the greater area of this profile (shaded in grey) is below the diagonal line of *Action* and *Reflection*, showing it to be a reflection-based learning style.

Profile Short Cuts	Opportunity for Learning
The short cut in the practical learning orientation may cause you to act on intuition, once you have gathered enough information and drawn conclusions. To others, you might be seen as a *thinker*, someone who is highly thoughtful, but also able to act quickly. You may be seen as impatient with the decision making and planning process. The result is that you may inadvertently compromise your effectiveness in managing both people and work. In a classroom, you may be impatient with too much structure, and vocalize your displeasure when there is too much time spent on action planning.	This learning style profile is a visual representation of a preferred way to learn. The low score in the practical orientation is non-preferred. Although this profile kite shape looks skewed, it is, in fact, very effective much of the time. However, at those times when the situation calls for more informed decision making and planning, this profile, and its resulting behaviours, are ineffective. For you to be able to deal with these novel situations, you need to stretch yourself beyond these preferred orientations into the one that you find more difficult, and possibly irritating.

Quadruple-Dominant Profile

Profile Shape	Profile Description
Learning Style Profile 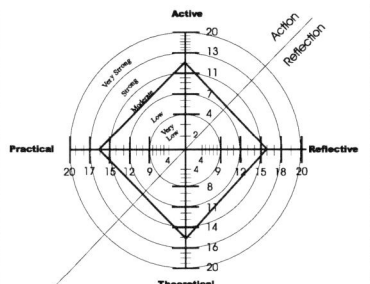 **Reflection/Action-Based Profile** 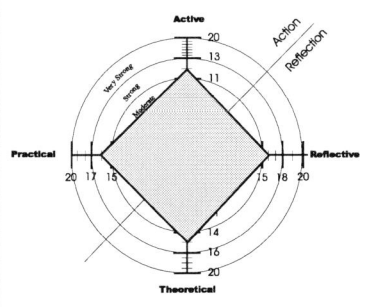	• **Strong/Very Strong score in the reflective orientation:** This means that you probably gather information readily. You are likely to be open to all sorts of information and ideas. • **Strong/Very Strong score in the theoretical orientation:** This means that you probably spend much time considering your options, and drawing conclusions on what you have considered. Even though you draw conclusions, the strong/very strong score in reflective orientation can cause a *wobble* between your desire for closure and your desire to remain open. • **Strong/Very Strong score in the practical orientation:** This means that you probably want practical and relevant solutions, and decisions that result in action. You may want to plan how to implement an action. • **Strong/Very Strong score in the active orientation:** This means that you are probably willing to take action quickly, having faith that it will work out. If it does not work out, you probably believe that you can figure it out as you go. In the reflection/action-based visual representation of this profile, the area of this profile (shaded in grey) is on both sides of the diagonal line of *Action* and *Reflection*, showing it to be a both a reflection- and an action-based learning style.

Profile Short Cuts	Opportunity for Learning
There are no short cuts in this profile, but that does not mean that this is always a good thing. The short cut is to spend too much time on each of the learning orientations, because all are equally important. To others, you might be seen as unable to make decisions, and always changing your mind. The result is that you may inadvertently compromise your effectiveness in managing both people and work. In a classroom, you may be irritated with the need for any closure, and vocalize your displeasure when there is any bias, or attention spent on any one thing.	This learning style profile is a visual representation of a preferred way to learn. There are no low scores, so what is non-preferred is paying little or no attention to any of the four learning orientations. Although this profile kite shape looks balanced, it is, in fact, ineffective some of the time. This profile helps you to see all points of view, but this can also allow you to spend too much time in all four learning orientations. You can easily get caught in wobbling from one learning orientation to another. This can make it difficult for you to make decisions and to act. You need to learn when to move from one orientation to another, and to stop second-guessing yourself.

LSQ Activity 3:
LSQ profile
under stress

1. To determine what happens to your learning orientation under stress, again complete the inventory on pages 2-4 of the *Blue Booklet*, but with a different perspective. When you read each statement this time, ask yourself the question: What would I do if I were under a lot of stress or pressure? **Circle** either **A** for agree or **D** for disagree on the *Response Form* below.

2. Once you have responded to all 80 statements, total your scores by counting the number of circled **A**s. When you have completed scoring, you will have four totals, one for each of the four learning orientations.

3. Use a different colour to record your *Under Stress* score on the *Normed Graph* on page 26. Record the colour you used in the legend, beside the words *Under Stress*.

Response Form

1. A D	2. A D	3. A D	4. A D	5. A D	6. A D	7. A D	8. A D
9. A D	10. A D	11. A D	12. A D	13. A D	14. A D	15. A D	16. A D
17. A D	18. A D	19. A D	20. A D	21. A D	22. A D	23. A D	24. A D
25. A D	26. A D	27. A D	28. A D	29. A D	30. A D	31. A D	32. A D
33. A D	34. A D	35. A D	36. A D	37. A D	38. A D	39. A D	40. A D
41. A D	42. A D	43. A D	44. A D	45. A D	46. A D	47. A D	48. A D
49. A D	50. A D	51. A D	52. A D	53. A D	54. A D	55. A D	56. A D
57. A D	58. A D	59. A D	60. A D	61. A D	62. A D	63. A D	64. A D
65. A D	66. A D	67. A D	68. A D	69. A D	70. A D	71. A D	72. A D
73. A D	74. A D	75. A D	76. A D	77. A D	78. A D	79. A D	80. A D
Active Score		Reflective Score		Theoretical Score		Practical Score	

LSQ Activity 4: Identifying strengths and weaknesses

1. On the next 2 pages of this Guide, read the lists of strengths and weaknesses for all four learning orientations.

2. Check off those strengths and weaknesses that describe your behaviour, especially when experiencing stressful situations.

3. Notice that your *strong* and *very strong* learning orientations have both strengths and weaknesses. Also, notice that you have some strengths in your *moderate, low* and *very low* learning orientations.

4. Review all four learning orientations, and select **1** strength, from **each** orientation, that describes your behaviour in solving problems, making decisions, and taking actions. List these **4 strengths** on the table on page 27 in the box labelled *Strengths*.

5. Review all 4 learning orientations, and select **1** weakness, from **each** learning style, that describes your behaviour in solving problems, making decisions, and taking actions. List these **4 weaknesses** on the table on page 27 in the box labelled *Weaknesses*.

Reflective Orientation Strengths	Reflective Orientation Weaknesses
❑ Takes care in doing things	❑ Is quiet and inward
❑ Is thorough	❑ Finds it difficult to participate actively in conversations
❑ Is methodical and systematic	❑ Takes a long time to make a decision, and even then is unsure of whether the decision is well-informed
❑ Is thoughtful about others, always considering their points of view	
❑ Listens to others	❑ Is too cautious
❑ Is open to diverse perspectives and new information	❑ Finds it difficult to take risks
❑ Always sees another point of view	❑ Is not assertive
❑ Enjoys gathering information	❑ Finds it difficult to make small talk
❑ Pays attention to detail	❑ Experiences paralysis from a need for more information
❑ Bases decisions on thorough analysis	❑ Writes many drafts of documents
❑ Avoids jumping to conclusions	❑ Finds tight deadlines worrisome
	❑ Gets irritated with people who rush things

Theoretical Orientation Strengths	Theoretical Orientation Weaknesses
❑ Is a logical thinker	❑ Has a low tolerance for uncertainty, disorder, and ambiguity
❑ Looks for patterns in problem solving	❑ Finds it difficult to tolerate subjective or *intuitive* reasoning
❑ Asks probing questions	
❑ Is objective	❑ Believes that people *should* and *must* do things
❑ Generates ideas and innovations	
❑ Is disciplined and structured in approaching situations	❑ Is highly critical of arguments that are not grounded in logic
❑ Is purposeful	❑ Has a low tolerance for a lack of purpose and direction
❑ Finds meaning, themes, and patterns in information and data	❑ Finds spontaneous people irrational
❑ Enjoys theory and models	❑ Finds it difficult to generate ideas on impulse
❑ Has strong value beliefs	❑ Is a perfectionist
❑ Is very organized	
❑ Identifies inconsistencies and weaknesses in situations	

Practical Orientation Strengths	Practical Orientation Weaknesses
❑ Is always ready to practice and test a new idea ❑ Is very practical ❑ Is application-focused ❑ Is realistic ❑ Gets to the point ❑ Enjoys techniques and tools that show people how to do things ❑ Makes ideas and innovations useable and workable ❑ Speaks his or her mind ❑ Generates practical ideas ❑ Keeps people on track	❑ Rejects ideas and concepts that have no obvious application or practicality ❑ Finds theory or principles useless ❑ Tries the first idea that seems to solve the problem, without considering other ideas or perspectives ❑ Is impatient with anyone who is indecisive ❑ Is task-oriented ❑ Is not people-oriented ❑ Is impatient ❑ Is insensitive to feelings

Active Orientation Strengths	Active Orientation Weaknesses
❑ Is flexible and open-minded to diverse perspectives and ideas ❑ Is ready to take action at any moment ❑ Enjoys new situations ❑ Is open to change ❑ Has faith that things will work out ❑ Accepts failure ❑ Is willing to participate actively ❑ Speaks his or her mind ❑ Has an orientation to the present, rather than the past or future ❑ Generates ideas spontaneously ❑ Is open to unusual ideas	❑ Takes action without thinking about the consequences ❑ Takes action without planning or preparation ❑ Is impulsive ❑ Takes unnecessary risks ❑ Needs attention and to be in the limelight ❑ Gets bored with implementation and maintenance ❑ Believes that formal procedures are restrictive and unnecessary ❑ Bases actions on intuition ❑ Feels uneasy with quiet people ❑ Gets bored with details

LSQ Activity 5:
Taking action

Reference
This activity is
based on the activity
on pages 17-26 of the
Beige Booklet.

1. Using the *Normed Graph* on page 26, recall the
   learning orientations that have your lowest scores.

2. Using the tables on the 2 previous pages, look at the
   tables for your lowest learning orientation scores. In
   the *Strengths* column, notice the strengths that you
   did not check off. The strengths that you did not
   check off are your areas for improvement. Decide
   whether these areas for improvement are sometimes
   (**S**) like you or rarely (**R**) like you, and record the letter
   S or **R** beside each statement.

3. Decide on which of these areas for improvement you
   are willing to work. Select **3** areas in which you think
   you are willing to make a commitment to improve.
   List them below:

4. From these 3 areas for improvement, select one area
   on which you will work for the next 6 months. Write
   this area of improvement as an action statement. For
   example, if you selected *Is realistic* as an area for
   improvement, you would write the action statement as
   "I am realistic." Write your action statement below:

   Action Statement:

5. Record your action statement on the table on
   page 27, in the box labeled *Action to be taken.*

LSQ Activity 6: Identifying excuses

Reference
This activity is based on the activity on pages 17-26 of the *Beige Booklet*.

This activity identifies the excuses that you will make in order to avoid working on your areas of weakness.

1. Review your weaker learning orientations. For those orientations, read the excuses listed in the *Beige Booklet*, and highlight the excuses that you use on a regular basis:

   - If you have a weakness in the **Activist** *(active)* learning orientation, read the excuses that are listed as a set of 6 short bullet items in the middle of page 18.

   - If you have a weakness in the **Reflector** *(reflective)* learning orientation, read the excuses that are listed as a set of 5 short bullet items at the bottom of page 20.

   - If you have a weakness in the **Theorist** *(theoretical)* learning orientation, read the excuses that are listed as a set of 4 short bullet items toward the top of page 23.

   - If you have a weakness in the **Pragmatist** *(practical)* learning orientation, read the excuses that are listed as a set of 5 short bullet items at the bottom of page 25.

2. Record your excuses from each learning orientation below.

3. Read your action statement, and review the excuses that you listed on the previous page. Select the excuses that you will probably use to not take action on your action statement. Record these excuses on the table on page 27, in the box labeled *Excuses for short cutting LSQ action item.*

4. Write your action item and excuses on a tent card. Use this tent card as a reminder to pay attention to taking action on your LSQ action item.

5. In both your personal life and the workplace, pay attention to the situations in which you use these excuses. These excuses are signals that tell you that you may be avoiding or short cutting a learning orientation.

LSQ Activity 7: Working on weaknesses

Reference
This activity is based on pages 17-26 of the *Beige Booklet.*

Action learning is another way in which to develop skills in your areas of weakness. For more information, see **Solving Real Problems in Real Time: Action Learning Guide** For more information on this Guide, see Section 3, *MHA Publications*, on page 58.

The *Beige Booklet* has several suggestions that you can read to decide how you might improve in your areas of weakness.

1. Review your weaker learning orientations. For those orientations, read the suggestions for improvement listed in the *Beige Booklet* and highlight the suggestions that might be the easiest for you to act upon:

   - If you have a weakness in the **Activist** (*active*) learning orientation, read the suggestions that are listed as a set of 5 long bullet items at the bottom of page 18 and the top of page 19.

   - If you have a weakness in the **Reflector** *(reflective)* learning orientation, read the suggestions that are listed as a set of 6 long bullet items starting at the top of page 21.

   - If you have a weakness in the **Theorist** *(theoretical)* learning orientation, read the suggestions that are listed as a set of 6 long bullet items at the bottom of page 23 and the top of page 24.

   - If you have a weakness in the **Pragmatist** *(practical)* learning orientation, read the suggestions that are listed as a set of 5 long bullet items starting at the top of page 26.

2. Read the other sections in the *Beige Booklet* that will help you to increase your strength in all learning orientations:

   - *Getting Help from Others*, pages 27-28
   - *Keeping a Learning Log*, pages 29-30

Research References

People who informed this Guide

This Guide is built on the ideas, and with the help, of others. The following is a list of people who informed the authors while they were writing this Guide.

David Perkins

David Perkins is senior research associate at the Harvard Graduate School of Education, and author of several books. He has written a provocative and informative book called **Outsmarting IQ: The Emerging Science of Learnable Intelligence**. In 1995, the authors read this book, and found that it explained many of the experiences they had in the classroom as well as their work with teams in organizations.

Reference
For information on books and articles that these researchers have written, see Section 3, *Guide References,* page 53.

David Kolb

David Kolb is a researcher in experiential learning and learning styles in the United States. David Kolb has developed the **Learning Style Inventory** (LSI). All learning cycles, including the one in this Guide, are based in some way on Kolb's *Experiential Learning Cycle.* There are four learning orientations in Kolb's model:

- *Reflective observation*, which is the same as the reflective orientation shown in this Guide

- *Abstract conceptualization*, which is the same as the theoretical orientation shown in this Guide

- *Active experimentation*, which is the same as the practical orientation shown in this Guide

- *Concrete experience*, which is the same as the active orientation shown in this Guide

Peter Honey and Alan Mumford

Peter Honey and Alan Mumford are researchers in action learning and learning styles in the United Kingdom. They have written the **Learning Styles Questionnaire (LSQ)** and **Capitalizing on Your Learning Style**, two booklets that are enclosed at the back of this Guide. When Honey and Mumford researched how managers solved problems, they found that managers consistently stated that they solved problems using the four actions listed below. They also assigned a learning style to each of these actions:

1. Have an experience: *Activist* learning style, which is the same as the active orientation

2. Review the experience: *Reflector* learning style, which is the same as the reflective orientation

3. Conclude from the experience: *Theorist* learning style, which is the same as the theoretical orientation

4. Plan the next steps: *Pragmatist* learning style, which is the same as the practical orientation

In 1996, the authors were first exposed to the LSQ, and found it to be very user-friendly, much better for use in organizations than Kolb's **Learning Style Inventory**. Since then, the authors have been using the LSQ with success both within classrooms and with teams. The *Learning Cycle* shown in this Guide is based on Honey and Mumford's work, as well as the work of other researchers.

Bernice McCarthy

Bernice McCarthy developed a way to design learning experiences that she calls the *4MAT Cycle*. The authors used her model to develop the *Design System* that is used throughout the instructions in this Guide.

Mardy Wheeler and Jeannie Marshall

Mardy Wheeler and Jeannie Marshall wrote an article called *The Trainer Type Inventory (TTI): Identifying Training Style Preferences*, in which they introduced an inventory for determining training styles. The authors read this article, and have tested the descriptors for the four training styles in a number of situations. The inventory was not easy to use, but the descriptors were validated.

Everyone Who Tested this Guide

The authors acknowledge the host of people who have helped us to develop this Guide by providing valuable feedback. They include:

- *MHA Learning Circle* participants, Calgary and Edmonton, Alberta, Canada

- Participants in courses at the University of Alberta, *Certificate for Adult Continuing Education*, Edmonton, Alberta, Canada

- Teams in both the public and private sector

- Dr. Sonia Herasymowych for her academic expertise

Guide References

Barret, F. J., *Creating Appreciative Learning Cultures,* Organizational **Dynamics**, Autumn 1995, Vol. 24, No. 2, pp. 36-49.

Brookfield, S. D. **Developing Critical Thinkers**. San Francisco: Jossey-Bass Inc., 1987.

Brookfield, S. D. **The Skillful Teacher**. San Francisco: Jossey-Bass Inc., 1990.

Brookfield, S. D. **Becoming a Critically Reflective Teacher**. San Francisco: Jossey-Bass Inc., 1995.

Brooks, Ann & Karen E. Watkins. **The Emerging Power of Action Inquiry Technologies**. San Francisco: Jossey-Bass Inc., 1994.

Burgoyne, J., M. Pedler & T. Boydell. **Towards the Learning Company: Concepts and Practices**. New York: McGraw-Hill, 1994.

Bushe, G. R., *Advances In Appreciative Inquiry As An Organization Development Intervention*, **Organization Development Journal**, Fall 1995, Vol. 13, No. 3, pp. 14-22.

Cooperrider, D. L., *An Interview With David Cooperrider On Appreciative Inquiry And The Future of OD*, **Organization Development Journal**, Fall 1995, Vol. 13, No. 3, pp. 5-13.

Cooperrider, D. L. & S. Srivasta. *Appreciative Inquiry In Organizational Life*, **Research in Organizational Change and Development**, 1987, Vol. 1, pp. 129-169.

Cooperrider, D. L. & S. Srivasta. **Appreciative Management and Leadership**. San Francisco: Jossey-Bass Inc., 1990.

De Geus, A. **The Living Company: Habits for Survival in A Turbulent Business Environment**. Boston: Harvard Business School Press, 1997.

Dilworth, R. L. *Action Learning*. **International Action Learning Seminar: Overheads, Summer 1996**. Salford, England: University of Salford, 1996.

Dixon, N. M. *Action Learning, Action Science and Learning New Skills*, **Industrial and Commercial Training**, 1990, Vol. 22, No. 4, pp. 10-16.

Froiland, P. *Action Learning: Taming Real Problems in Real Time*, **Training**, January, 1994, pp. 27-34.

Hammond, S. A. **The Thin Book of Appreciative Inquiry**. Plano, Texas: CSS Publishing Co., 1996.

Hammond, S. A. & C. Royal. **Lessons From the Field: Applying Appreciative Inquiry**. Plano, Texas: Practical Press Inc., 1998.

Harpaz Y. & G. Vennor. A presentation at the *1999 International Thinking Conference*. Edmonton, Alberta, Canada: July 1999.

Herasymowych, M. & H. Senko. **Solving Real Problems in Real Time: Action-Learning Fieldbook**. Calgary, Alberta, Canada: MHA Institute Inc., 2003.

Herasymowych, M. & H. Senko. **Navigating Through Complexity: Systems Thinking Guide**. Calgary, Alberta, Canada: MHA Institute Inc., 2002.

Herrmann, N. **The Creative Brain**. Lake Lure, North Carolina: The Ned Herrmann Group, 1996.

Herrmann, N. **The Whole Brain Business Book: Unlocking the Power of Whole Brain Thinking in organizations and Individuals**. Toronto: McGraw-Hill, 1996.

Honey, P. & Mumford, A. *Learning Styles Questionnaire: Facilitator Guide*. King of Prussia, Pennsylvania, USA: Organization Design and Development, Inc., 1986, 1989, 1995.

Honey, P. & Mumford, A. *Learning Styles Questionnaire*. King of Prussia, Pennsylvania, USA: Organization Design and Development, Inc., 1986, 1989, 1995.

Honey, P. & Mumford, A. *Capitalizing on Your Learning Style*. King of Prussia, PA, USA: Organization Design and Development, Inc., 1986, 1989, 1995.

Kolb, D. A. *LSI Learning Style Inventory User's Guide*. Boston: McBer & Company, 1986.

McCarthy, B. **The 4Mat System: Teaching Learning Styles With Right/Left Mode Techniques**. Chicago: Excel, 1980.

McCarthy, B. **About Learning**. Amherst, New York: Prometheus Books, 1996.

Margerison, C. *Action Learning for Managers*, **International Action Learning Seminar: Papers and Additional Papers, Summer 1996**. Salford, England: University of Salford, 1996.

Marsick, V. J. *Action Learning and Reflection in the Workplace*, pp. 23-46 in Mezirow, J., Fostering **Critical Reflection in Adulthood**. San Francisco: Jossey-Bass, 1990.

Marsick, V. J. & L. Cederholm. *Developing Leadership in International Managers — An Urgent Challenge*, **The Columbia Journal of World Business**, Winter 1988, Vol. 22, No. 4, reprint.

Marsick, V. J., L. Cederholm, E. Turner & T. Pearson. *Action-Reflection Learning*, **Training and Development**, 1992, Vol. 46, No. 8, pp. 63-66.

Merriam, S. B. & R.S. Caffarella. **Learning in Adulthood: A Comprehensive Guide**. San Francisco: Jossey-Bass Inc., 1999.

Mezirow, J. Jack Mezirow interview: *Transformative Learning*. Video. Richmond, Virginia: Virginia Commonwealth University, 1994.

Mintzberg, H. *The Manager's Job: Folklore and Fact*, **Harvard Business Review**, March-April 1990, pp. 163-176.

Mumford, A. *Learning Styles and Learning Skills*, **Journal of Management Development**, 1982, Vol. 1, No. 2.

Mumford, A. **Management Development: Strategies for Action**. London: Institute of Personnel Management, 1993.

Mumford, A. A talk given at the *International Action Learning Seminar, Summer 1996*. Salford, England: July-August 1996.

Nummela Caine, R. & G. Caine. **Education on the Edge of Possibility**. Alexandria, Virginia: Association for Supervision and Curriculum Development, 1997.

Nummela Caine, R. & G. Caine. **Unleashing the Power of Perceptual Change: The Potential of Brain-Based Teaching**. Alexandria, Virginia: Association for Supervision and Curriculum Development, 1997.

Pedler, M. **Action Learning in Practice**. M. Pedler, ed. London: Gower, 2nd Ed., 1991.

Pedler, M. **Action Learning for Managers**. London: Lemos & Crane, 1996.

Pedler, M. A talk given at the *International Action Learning Seminar, Summer 1996*. Salford, England: July-August 1996.

Pedler, M., J. Burgoyne & T. Boydell. **The Learning Company: A Strategy for Sustainable Development**. London: McGraw-Hill Book Company, 1996.

Pedler, M & K. Aspinwall. **'Perfect plc': The Purpose and Practice of Organizational Learning**. London: McGraw-Hill Book Company, 1996.

Perkins, D. **Outsmarting IQ: The Emerging Science of Learnable Intelligence**. Toronto: The Free Press, 1995.

Pert, C. **Molecules of Emotion: Why You Feel the Way You Feel**. New York: Scribner, 1997.

Redding, J. C. & R.F. Catalanello. **Strategic Readiness: The Making of The Learning Organization**. San Francisco: Jossey-Bass, 1994.

Revans, R. A talk given at the *International Action Learning Seminar, Summer 1996*. Salford, England: July-August 1996.

Revans, R. *1945-1985: Forty Years of Action Learning. International Action Learning Seminar: Papers and Additional Papers, Summer 1996*. Salford, England: University of Salford, 1996.

Revans, R. **ABC of** Action **Learning: Empowering Managers To Act and To Learn from Action**. London, England: Lemos & Crane, 1998.

Schein, E. H. *How Can Organizations Learn Faster? The Challenge of the Green Room,* **Sloan Management Review**, Winter 1993, pp. 85-92.

Schein, E. H. *Organizational and Managerial Culture as a Facilitator or Inhibitor of Organizational Learning*, **Society of Learning Website**, http://learning.mit.edu/res/wp/pubs.html, 1994.

Schein, E. H. *Kurt Lewin's Change Theory in the Field and in the Classroom*, **Society of Learning Website**, http://learning.mit.edu/res/wp/pubs.html, 1995.

Senge, P.M., C. Roberts, R.B. Ross, B.J. Smith & A. Kleiner. **The Fifth Discipline Fieldbook**. New York: Doubleday, 1994.

Senge, P.M., A. Kleiner, C. Roberts, R.B. Ross, G. Roth & B. Smith. **The Dance of Change: The Challenges To Sustaining Momentum in learning Organizations**. New York: Doubleday, 1999.

Watkins, K. E. & V.J. Marsick. **Sculpting the Learning Organization**. San Francisco: Jossey-Bass Inc., 1993.

Watkins, K. E. & V.J. Marsick. A seminar, and handouts, given at the *University of Alberta, 1995*. Edmonton, Alberta, Canada, 1995.

Weinstein, K. **Action Learning: A Journey in Discovery and Development**. London, England: HarperCollins Publishers, 1995.

Wenger, W. & Richard Poe. **The Einstein Factor: A Proven Method for Increasing Your Intelligence**. Rocklin, California, USA: Prima Publishing, 1996.

MHA InfoMine Publications

MHA Institute Inc. is a leading-edge research and development company that focuses on building organizations' capacity to meet the challenges of the 21st Century. MHA consultants work with clients to help them learn at the speed of change. They research, field-test, and evaluate a variety of thinking and learning processes to identify those that produce exceptional and sustainable results. Because they are connected internationally with leading researchers in the field of thinking and learning, they have access to a wealth of knowledge and experience, including their own.

Since 1994, MHA Institute has been publishing *InfoMine* as a way to inform people about its consultants' research interests. The purpose of *InfoMine* is simply to pique your interest about how people learn, and how to create sustainable change. *InfoMine* is published every two months, and is complimentary. You can find all of the back issues on the MHA Institute website at **www.mhainstitute.ca**, under the *Newsletters* button.

Useful Contacts

Associations

Join the *International Foundation for Action Learning (IFAL)*:

- Worldwide (IFAL): p.wright@lancaster.ac.uk
- In Canada (IFAL Canada): pasmith@tlainc.com

Learning styles

You can order extra copies of the two booklets called *Learning Style Questionnaire* and *Capitalizing on Your Learning Style*, as well as a *Facilitator's Guide*, from:

- In Canada: Organizational Learning Resources, 1-888-889-2184 (Toll-free)
- In the United States: HRDQ, 1-800-633-4533 (Toll-free)

MHA Institute is developing a set of lesson plans for administering and interpreting learning styles. Continue to check the MHA Institute website to stay in touch with progress: **www.mhainstitute.ca**

Thinking styles

For more information on whole-brain thinking and the Herrmann Brain Dominance Instrument (HBDI), contact:

- In Canada: **www.mhainstitute.ca**, and **www3.sympatico.ca/camiq**
- In the United States: **www.hbdi.com**

Support systems

Over time, MHA Institute plans to develop support systems for every Guide sold. Continue to check the MHA website to stay in touch with any progress: **www.mhainstitute.ca**

MHA Institute Inc.

To order these Guides, check out **www.mhainstitute.ca**

Leadership Through Learning Series

- Navigating Through Complexity: Systems Thinking Guide
- Complexity, Relationships, and Strange Loops: Reflexive Practice Guide
- Corporate Culture and Organizational Change: Strategic Practice Guide

Learning in Action Series

- Solving Real Problems in Real Time: Action Learning Guide
- Revving Up Thinking and Learning: Course Design Guide

Management Learning Series

- Leading for Optimal Performance: Managing Performance Guide

InfoMine Newsletters: Back Issues

Author! Author!

Marilyn Herasymowych

Marilyn Herasymowych, an author and applied research consultant, is the founder and a managing partner of MHA Institute Inc. Her interest lies in developing healthy and creative communities of learning that are capable of generating novel forms of knowledge. Using a scientific perspective, Marilyn researches emerging theories and methods, in order to develop user-friendly tools that people can apply in daily work. Marilyn has a BSc in Biochemistry, a PDAD in Education, and a Master of Continuing Education degree, specializing in *Learning in the Workplace*. Marilyn also has a Doctorate in Professional Studies, specializing in *Emergent Leadership Through Learning*.

Henry Senko

Henry Senko, an author and applied research consultant, is a founder and a managing partner of MHA Institute Inc. His specialty lies in working with managers and teams to design work processes that incorporate learning as a part of daily work routines. Since 1992, Henry has been focusing on learning in the workplace, consulting with individuals, teams, and organizations in both the public and private sectors. Henry has a Master of Business Administration degree, with a focus on *Emergent Strategy in Organizations*. Henry also has a Doctorate in Professional Studies, specializing in *Sustainability and Organizational Design*.

LEARNING STYLES
QUESTIONNAIRE

PETER HONEY AND ALAN MUMFORD

LEARNING STYLES QUESTIONNAIRE

Developed by Peter Honey, PhD and Alan Mumford, DLitt

The *Learning Styles Questionnaire* (LSQ) is designed to help you discover your preferred learning style(s). Over the years you probably have developed learning habits that help you benefit more from some experiences than from others. Because you may be unaware of these habits, this Questionnaire will help you to pinpoint your learning preferences. This information will put you in a better position to select learning experiences that suit your style or strengthen your style to accommodate other types of learning.

There is no time limit for completing the LSQ. The accuracy of the results depends on how objectively you can compare yourself to the following 80 statements. Please circle your responses on the Response Form that follows. Press hard using a ball-point pen; your answers will be recorded on the sheet beneath it. There are no right or wrong answers. If you *agree* more than you disagree with a statement, circle the A. If you *disagree* more than you agree, circle the D. Be sure you circle only one response for each item.

To make it easier to work with the Questionnaire pages, you can remove these pages at the perforated lines. *Do not remove the Response Form at this time.*

Please turn the page and begin.

QUESTIONNAIRE

Directions: If you *agree* more than you disagree with a statement, circle the A. If you *disagree* more than you agree, circle the D. Please place all of your responses on the Response Form.

1. I often act without considering the possible consequences.

2. I believe that formal procedures and policies restrict people.

3. I like the type of work where I have time for thorough preparation and implementation.

4. I listen to other people's points of view before putting my own forward.

5. I have strong beliefs about what is right and wrong, good and bad.

6. I tend to solve problems using a step-by-step approach.

7. I have a reputation for saying what I think, simply and directly.

8. What matters most is whether something works in practice.

9. I often find that actions based on feelings are as sound as those based on careful thought and analysis.

10. I actively seek out new experiences.

11. I take care with the interpretation of data available to me and avoid jumping to conclusions.

12. In discussions I enjoy watching the maneuvering of the other participants.

13. I regularly question people about their basic assumptions.

14. I practice self-discipline such as watching my diet, getting regular exercise, sticking to a fixed routine, etc.

15. When I hear about a new idea or approach, I immediately start working out how to apply it in practice.

16. I accept and stick to laid down procedures and policies as long as I regard them as an efficient way of getting the job done.

17. I enjoy being the one who talks a lot.

18. I thrive on the challenge of tackling something new and different.

19. I pay meticulous attention to detail before coming to a conclusion.

20. I am always interested in finding out what people think.

Response Form

Directions: Record your responses to the Questionnaire on this page. Circle **A** if you **agree** more than you disagree; circle **D** if you **disagree** more than you agree.

1	2	3	4	5	6	7	8
A D	A D	A D	A D	A D	A D	A D	A D
9	10	11	12	13	14	15	16
A D	A D	A D	A D	A D	A D	A D	A D
17	18	19	20	21	22	23	24
A D	A D	A D	A D	A D	A D	A D	A D
25	26	27	28	29	30	31	32
A D	A D	A D	A D	A D	A D	A D	A D
33	34	35	36	37	38	39	40
A D	A D	A D	A D	A D	A D	A D	A D
41	42	43	44	45	46	47	48
A D	A D	A D	A D	A D	A D	A D	A D
49	50	51	52	53	54	55	56
A D	A D	A D	A D	A D	A D	A D	A D
57	58	59	60	61	62	63	64
A D	A D	A D	A D	A D	A D	A D	A D
65	66	67	68	69	70	71	72
A D	A D	A D	A D	A D	A D	A D	A D
73	74	75	76	77	78	79	80
A D	A D	A D	A D	A D	A D	A D	A D

Learning Styles Questionnaire

21. I get along best with logical, analytical people and less well with spontaneous, "irrational" people.

22. I do not like disorganized things and prefer to fit things into a coherent pattern.

23. In discussions I like to get straight to the point.

24. I prefer to try things out to see if they work in practice.

25. I enjoy fun-loving, spontaneous people.

26. I tend to be open about how I am feeling.

27. I prefer to have as many sources of information as possible — the more data to think over, the better.

28. I take pride in doing a thorough job.

29. I like to relate my actions to a general principle.

30. I tend to have distant, rather formal relationships with people at work.

31. I tend to be attracted to techniques such as network analysis, flow charts, branching programs, contingency planning, etc.

32. I tend to judge people's ideas on their practical merits.

33. I prefer to respond to events on a spontaneous, flexible basis rather than plan things out in advance.

34. Quiet, thoughtful people tend to make me feel uneasy.

35. I like to reach a decision carefully after weighing many alternatives.

36. It worries me if I have to rush a piece of work to meet a tight deadline.

37. I believe that rational, logical thinking should win the day.

38. Flippant people who do not take things seriously enough usually irritate me.

39. In meetings I put forward practical, realistic ideas.

40. I can often see better, more practical ways to get things done.

41. It is more important to enjoy the present moment than to think about the past or future.

42. In discussions I usually produce a lot of spontaneous ideas.

43. I often get irritated with people who want to rush things.

44. I think that decisions based on a thorough analysis of all the information are sounder than those based on intuition.

45. I tend to be a perfectionist.

46. I can often see inconsistencies and weaknesses in other people's arguments.

47. I think written reports should be short and to the point.

48. I like people who approach things realistically rather than theoretically.

49. More often than not, rules are there to be broken.

50. On balance I talk more than I listen.

51. I prefer to stand back from a situation and consider all the perspectives.

52. I tend to discuss specific things with people rather than to engage in social discussion.

53. I find it difficult to produce ideas on impulse.

54. I prefer to reach answers via a logical approach.

55. In discussions I get impatient with irrelevancies and digressions.

56. I believe in coming to the point immediately.

57. I am attracted more to novel, unusual ideas than to practical ones.

58. When things go wrong, I am happy to shrug it off and "put it down to experience."

59. If I have a report to write I tend to produce a lot of drafts before sending it to the final version.

60. I like to ponder many alternatives before making up my mind.

61. In discussions with people I often find I am the most dispassionate and objective.

62. I like to be able to relate current actions to a longer-term, bigger picture.

63. I do whatever is expedient to get the job done.

64. I tend to reject wild, spontaneous ideas as being impractical.

65. I find the formality of having specific objectives and plans stifling.

66. I am usually one of the people who puts life into a party.

67. In discussions I am more likely to adopt a "low profile" than to take the lead and do most of the talking.

68. It is best to think carefully before taking action.

69. I tend to be tough on people who find it difficult to adopt a logical approach.

70. I prefer exploring the basic assumptions, principles, and theories underpinning things and events.

71. Most times I believe the end justifies the means.

72. I do not mind hurting people's feelings as long as the job gets done.

73. I quickly get bored with methodical, detailed work.

74. I enjoy the drama and excitement of a crisis situation.

75. On balance I do the listening rather than the talking.

76. I am careful not to jump to conclusions too quickly.

77. I like meetings to be run methodically, sticking to a laid down agenda, etc.

78. I steer clear of subjective or ambiguous topics.

79. In discussions I often find I am the realist, keeping people to the point and avoiding wild speculations.

80. People often find me insensitive to their feelings.

Scoring the Questionnaire

The LSQ consists of 80 items. You were to determine whether you mostly agreed or disagreed with each statement. If you *agreed* more than you disagreed, you circled A on the Response Form for that item. If you *disagreed* more than you agreed, you circled D. Please follow the steps below to score your responses.

1. Remove the two-part Response Form by separating it from the booklet at the perforated line.

2. Separate the Response Form from the attached Scoring Form.

3. The scoring chart has been divided into four sets of two columns each. For Columns 1 and 2 add the number of ✓ that have been *circled* and place the sum in the space provided at the bottom of Column 2. Do the same for Columns 3 and 4, 5 and 6, 7 and 8.

4. Four learning styles have been identified by this instrument: Activist, Reflector, Theorist, and Pragmatist. You now have a score for each of these styles.

5. Transfer the Total Score for each of the four learning styles to the diagram on page 9.

6. For an in-depth interpretation of your scores and the four learning styles, refer to the accompanying workbook, *Capitalizing on Your Learning Style*.

Plotting Your Scores

A useful, pictorial way to show your results is to plot your four learning style scores on the diagram below. Put a small mark on each arm at the point that represents your score for that style, then connect the four scores with a *solid* line. (You should have an irregular diamond shape when all four points are connected. See the inset box below for a sample diagram.)

You may wish to compare your scores to those of others who have taken the LSQ. General norms based on the scores of more than 3,500 people can be found on page 2 of the companion workbook, *Capitalizing on Your Learning Style*. Normative scores for specific groups of LSQ respondents can be found on pages 3–4. Begin by locating the group you would like to use for comparison. Then determine which aspect of the data you would like to use; i.e., the top 30%, bottom 30%, mean scores, etc.

Once you have selected the set of norms you would like to compare with your own, simply plot the scores on the diagram below with a *dotted* line. Any of your scores that coincide with or exceed the dotted line indicate a strong preference for that style compared with those in your selected comparison group.

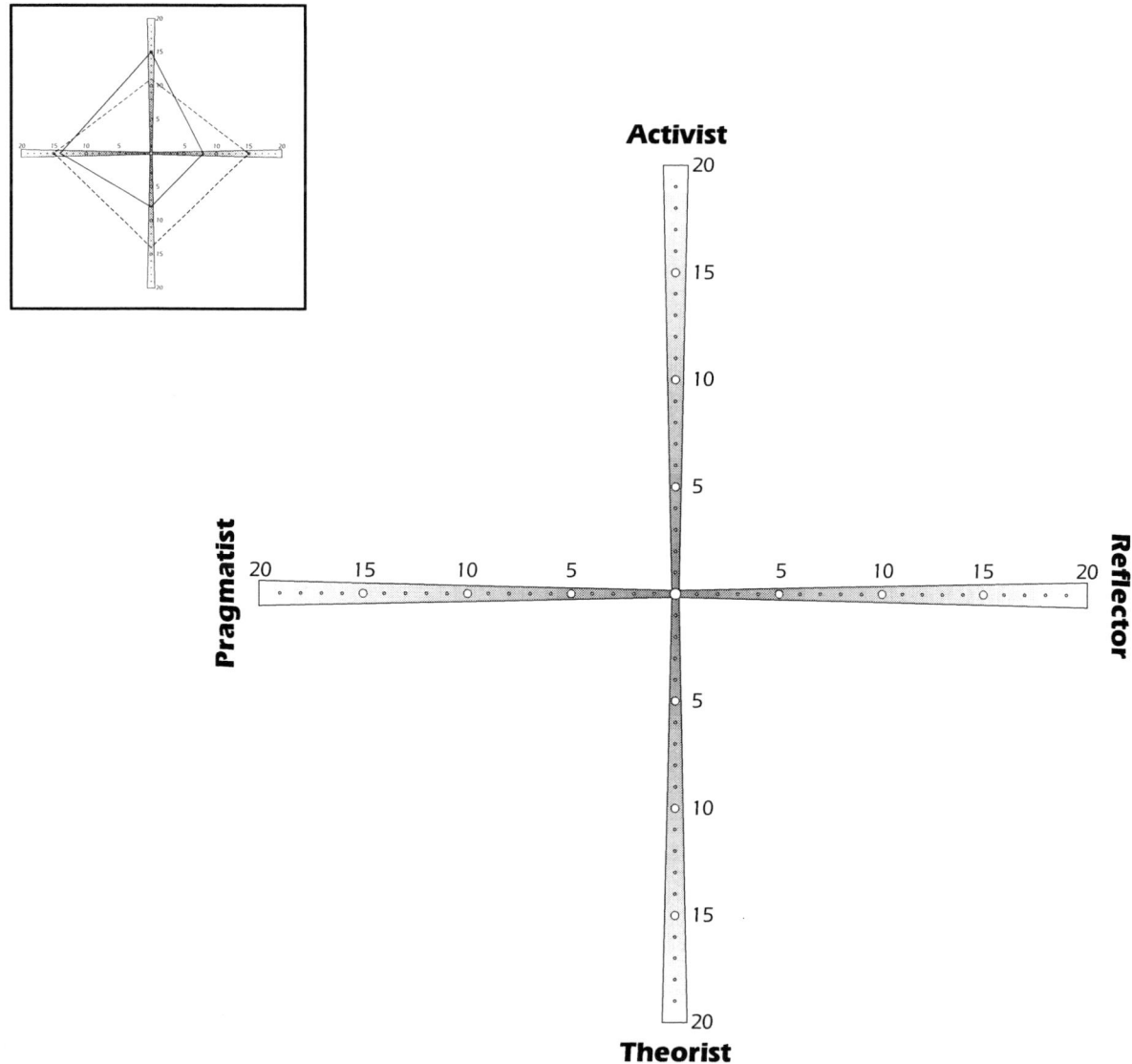

Learning and the Importance of the Individual

Learning is such a fundamental process that many people take it for granted, assuming that by the time they are adults they have learned how to learn and need no further assistance with the process. Yet it is patently clear that people vary not just in their learning skills but also in their learning styles. Why otherwise might two people, matched for age, intelligence and need, and exposed to the same learning opportunity, react so differently? One person emerges enthusiastic, able to articulate and implement what has been learned. The other claims it was a waste of time and that nothing has been learned.

Why, with other factors apparently common, does one person learn while another does not? The answer lies in our differing preferences for *how* we learn — our *learning style*. Identifying your learning style is an important tool both in helping you select the best learning opportunities for you and in getting the most out of any learning opportunity.

A Definition of Learning

Learning has happened when we can demonstrate that we know something we didn't know before (insights and realizations as well as facts) and/or when we can do something we couldn't do before (skills).

We learn in two substantially different ways. Sometimes we learn through formal, structured activities such as lectures, case studies, and books. Other times we learn from personal experiences, often in an unconscious, unstructured way. For most of us, learning dedicated to the acquisition of knowledge is both more familiar and more straightforward than experiential learning. It is more familiar not because we necessarily do it more often, but because most people associate the word "learning" with the acquisition of facts rather than with the messier process of learning from day-to-day experiences.

Our learning style preferences have implications for both types of learning.

8

The Learning Cycle

Learning is a lifelong process. We can never really say that we have learned all there is to learn or that our learning is complete. This continuous process is rather like the coils in a spring.

Learning is a Lifelong Process

Each coil encompasses four distinct stages of a learning cycle. The four stages (Experiencing, Reviewing, Concluding, and Planning) are mutually supportive. None is fully effective as a learning procedure on its own. Each stage plays an equally important part in the total learning process (although the time spent on each may vary considerably).

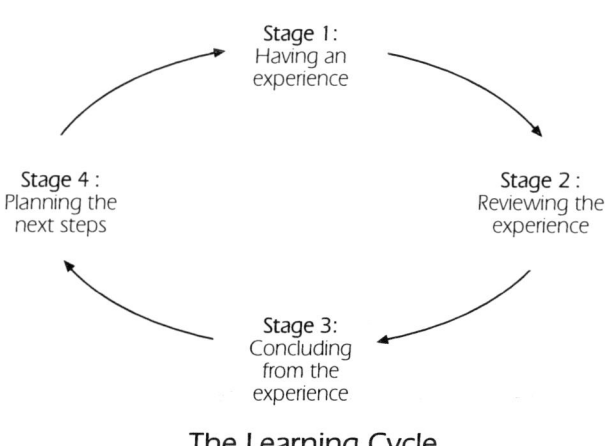

The Learning Cycle

A learner can start anywhere in the cycle because each stage feeds into the next — it is a continuous process. You could, for example, start by acquiring some information (Stage 2), think about it before reaching some conclusions (Stage 3), and decide how to apply it (Stage 4) and then test that application (Stage 1).

Or, you could start at Stage 4 by choosing to learn a new process. Using the process would then be Stage 1, followed by reviewing how it worked (Stage 2), reaching conclusions (Stage 3), and modifying the process in light of the experience (Stage 4).

Over time, most of us develop preferences for certain stages in the learning cycle over others. Learning styles are the key to understanding these different preferences.

Learning Styles

Your attitudes and behaviors toward learning develop into a preferred way of learning — your learning style. Most people are unaware of their learning style preferences. They just know vaguely that they feel more comfortable with, and learn more from, some activities than others.

Like any other behavioral style, learning style develops through repetition of strategies and tactics found to be successful and discontinuation of those that are not. As we mature, our learning styles tend to be strengthened as we gravitate towards work and life experiences that are compatible with our learning preferences. However, the stronger our learning style(s) becomes, the greater emphasis we may come to place on some stages of the learning cycle to the detriment of others.

On the next four pages, you will find a description of four learning styles:

- **Activist**
- **Reflector**
- **Theorist**
- **Pragmatist**

The *Learning Styles Questionnaire* items that you responded to measured your preference for these styles. Each of the four learning styles corresponds to a stage on the continuous learning cycle, which has important implications for being an effective learner.

This report is a starting point for you to understand your learning style. Please refer to the separate workbook, *Capitalizing on Your Learning Style*, for a more in-depth description and interpretation of your scores as well as checklists, activities, and recommendations for strengthening all of the learning styles.

Learning Styles — General Descriptions

The following is a brief description of the four general learning styles. Please refer to the workbook, *Capitalizing on Your Learning Style*, for a fuller description and interpretation of your scores.

Activists

Activists involve themselves fully and without bias in new experiences. They enjoy the here and now and are happy to be dominated by immediate experiences. They are open-minded, not skeptical, and this tends to make them enthusiastic about anything new. Their philosophy is: "I'll try anything once." Activists tend to act first and consider the consequences later. Their days are filled with activity. They tackle problems by brainstorming. As soon as the excitement from one activity has died down, they are busy looking for the next. They tend to thrive on the challenge of new experiences but are bored with implementation and longer-term consolidation. Activists are gregarious people, constantly involving themselves with others, but in doing so they seek to center all activities around themselves.

Reflectors

Reflectors like to stand back to ponder experiences and observe them from many different perspectives. They collect data, both firsthand and from others, and prefer to think about it thoroughly before coming to any conclusion. The thorough collection and analysis of data about experiences and events are what count, so they tend to postpone reaching definitive conclusions for as long as possible. Their philosophy is to be cautious. Reflectors are thoughtful people who like to consider all possible angles and implications before making a move. They prefer to take a back seat in meetings and discussions. They enjoy observing other people in action. They listen to others and get the drift of the discussion before making their own points. Reflectors tend to adopt a low profile and have a slightly distant, tolerant, unruffled air about them. When they act, it is part of a larger picture, which includes the past as well as the present, and others' observations as well as their own.

11

Theorists

Theorists adapt and integrate observations into complex but logically sound theories. They think problems through in a vertical, step-by-step, logical way. They assimilate disparate facts into coherent theories. They tend to be perfectionists who will not rest easily until things are tidy and fit into a rational scheme. Theorists like to analyze and synthesize. They are interested in basic assumptions, principles, theories, models, and systems thinking. Their philosophy prizes rationality and logic. "If it's logical, it's good." Questions they frequently ask are: "Does it make sense?" "How does this fit with that?" "What are the basic assumptions?" Theorists tend to be detached, analytical and dedicated to rational objectivity rather than anything subjective or ambiguous. Their approach to problems is consistently logical. This is their "mental set" and they rigidly reject anything that does not fit with it. They prefer to maximize certainty and feel uncomfortable with subjective judgments, lateral thinking, and anything flippant.

Pragmatists

Pragmatists are interested in trying out ideas, theories, and techniques to see if they work in practice. They positively search out new ideas and take the first opportunity to experiment with applications. They are the type of people who return from conferences and workshops brimming with new ideas they want to try out in practice. Pragmatists like to get on with things and act quickly and confidently on ideas that attract them. They tend to be impatient with ruminating and open-ended discussions. They are essentially practical, down-to-earth people who like making practical decisions and solving problems. Pragmatists see problems and opportunities as a challenge. Their philosophy is: "There is always a better way," and "if it works, it's good."

Learning Style Strengths

No one style is better than another. However, the strengths of a particular style may be more important for learning in one type of situation than another. Since you do not always have a choice of learning situations, it is important to develop strengths in all four learning styles so you can be most effective.

Although you probably have a dominant learning style, you have strengths in other areas as well. Place a checkmark in the boxes next to any item you perceive to be a strength for you.

Activist

Strengths

☐ Flexible and open-minded

☐ Ready to take action

☐ Likes to be exposed to new situations

☐ Optimistic about anything new and therefore unlikely to resist change

Reflector

Strengths

☐ Thorough and methodical

☐ Thoughtful

☐ Good at listening to others and assimilating information

☐ Rarely jumps to conclusions

Theorist

Strengths

☐ Logical, vertical thinker

☐ Rational and objective

☐ Good at asking probing questions

☐ Disciplined approach

Pragmatist

Strengths

☐ Eager to test things out in practice

☐ Practical, down to earth, realistic

☐ Business-like — gets straight to the point

☐ Technique-oriented

Learning Style Weaknesses

Understanding the weaknesses of your preferred learning style(s) will help you filter out activities that might make your learning less effective. Place a checkmark in the boxes next to any item you perceive to be a weakness for you. These are the behaviors you want to work on first when expanding your learning styles repertoire.

Activist

Weaknesses

☐ Tendency to do too much themselves and hog the limelight

☐ Often takes unnecessary risks

☐ Rushes into action without sufficient preparation

☐ Gets bored with implementation/consolidation

Reflector

Weaknesses

☐ Tendency to hold back from direct participation

☐ Slow to make up their minds and reach a decision

☐ Tendency to be too cautious and not take enough risks

☐ Not assertive or particularly forth-coming; does not make small talk

Theorist

Weaknesses

☐ Restricted in lateral thinking

☐ Low tolerance for uncertainty, disorder, and ambiguity

☐ Intolerant of anything subjective or intuitive

☐ Full of "shoulds, oughts, and musts"

Pragmatist

Weaknesses

☐ Tendency to reject anything without an obvious application

☐ Not very interested in theory or basic principles

☐ Impatient with indecision

☐ On balance, task-oriented not people-oriented

REFLECTION QUESTIONS

1. Do you agree with your LSQ results? What information do you have to support your view from past learning experiences? What information do you have from other people confirming or contradicting your view?

2. Describe two of your most helpful learning experiences. What were they and what made them helpful?

3. Describe two of your least helpful learning experiences. What were they and what made them unhelpful?

4. Which learning style(s) do you think you need to improve the most?

CAPITALIZING ON YOUR LEARNING STYLE

The explanation of this learning model and interpretation of your scores are minimally presented in this booklet. Please refer to the expanded material in the accompanying workbook, *Capitalizing on Your Learning Style*.

About This Product

About the Authors

Peter Honey, PhD is a psychologist who began work as an independent management consultant in 1969. He specializes in all aspects of human behavior and its consequences. He regularly conducts programs on developing interactive skills, creative thinking, and problem solving. Peter is a member of the British Psychological Society and the Institute of Management Consultants.

Alan Mumford, DLitt is a UK-based consultant, researcher, and author whose main focus is on how senior executives learn. His work takes him to countries as diverse as Nepal, Australia, South Africa, Finland, and the United States. His prime interests are covered in his recent books, *How Managers Can Develop Managers* and *Learning at the Top*.

About the HRDQ Research and Development Team

HRDQ's commitment to theory-driven products and services starts with our Research and Development Team. Our development process is the backbone of all of our products and services, whether we're creating off-the-shelf learning instruments or custom interventions. In addition to holding advanced degrees, all of our team members are trained in behavioral science research techniques and have practical training-room experience, so you can be assured that the products you are purchasing have been professionally developed and scientifically tested.

For more information about the HRDQ Research and Development Team, please visit our website at www.hrdq.com.

About HRDQ

HRDQ puts theory to work through the development of high-quality, well-researched training programs, assessments, games, and other learning resources for individuals, teams, and organizations. For over 25 years, HRDQ has distributed these products through its catalog and a worldwide network of distributors. HRDQ also offers consulting services, custom-developed products, and organizational analyses.

Welcome to a better way to train.

With the experiential solutions of HRDQ, you'll engage and involve your learners. And research shows that's what makes the difference. According to the NTL Institute for Applied Behavioral Sciences, people remember just half of what they hear in a lecture, while they retain up to 75% if they can "practice by doing."

Building a model with teammates. Taking a skills assessment. Role-playing. Action planning. It's all part of the HRDQ experience. For more than 25 years, we've helped thousands of leading organizations improve performance and solve business challenges with learning solutions based on our unique Experiential Learning Model™. And we want to help you do the same.

> " **Learning is not a spectator sport.** Learners do not learn much by just sitting and listening, memorizing prepackaged assignments, and spitting out answers. They must talk about what they are learning, write about it, relate it to past experiences, apply it to their daily lives. They must make what they learn part of themselves. "

A.W. CHICKERING AND Z.F. GAMSON
"SEVEN PRINCIPLES FOR GOOD PRACTICE"
AAHE BULLETIN, 1987

rev 06.07

 Call on us today. We'll help you find the right products to match your training needs.
800.633.4533

Learning Styles Questionnaire
CODE 1205S
may be ordered from:

2002 Renaissance Boulevard #100
King of Prussia, PA 19406-2756
800.633.4533 ▪ www.hrdq.com

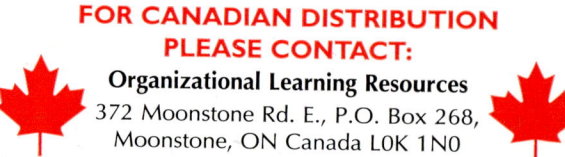

**FOR CANADIAN DISTRIBUTION
PLEASE CONTACT:**
Organizational Learning Resources
372 Moonstone Rd. E., P.O. Box 268,
Moonstone, ON Canada L0K 1N0
Tel: 888-889-2184   Fax: 888-889-2183
www.olresources.ca

EN-02-NV-08

CAPITALIZING ON YOUR
LEARNING STYLE

Reflector

Pragmatist

Theorist

Activist

PETER HONEY AND ALAN MUMFORD

CAPITALIZING ON YOUR LEARNING STYLE

Developed by Peter Honey, PhD and Alan Mumford, DLitt

Contents

About This Product

About the Authors

Peter Honey, PhD is a psychologist who began work as an independent management consultant in 1969. He specializes in all aspects of human behavior and its consequences. He regularly conducts programs on developing interactive skills, creative thinking, and problem solving. Peter is a member of the British Psychological Society and the Institute of Management Consultants.

Alan Mumford, DLitt is a UK-based consultant, researcher, and author whose main focus is on how senior executives learn. His work takes him to countries as diverse as Nepal, Australia, South Africa, Finland, and the United States. His prime interests are covered in his recent books, *How Managers Can Develop Managers* and *Learning at the Top*.

About the HRDQ Research and Development Team

HRDQ's commitment to theory-driven products and services starts with our Research and Development Team. Our development process is the backbone of all of our products and services, whether we're creating off-the-shelf learning instruments or custom interventions. In addition to holding advanced degrees, all of our team members are trained in behavioral science research techniques and have practical training-room experience, so you can be assured that the products you are purchasing have been professionally developed and scientifically tested.

For more information about the HRDQ Research and Development Team, please visit our website at www.hrdq.com.

About HRDQ

HRDQ is a leader in the development of experiential learning solutions that improve the performance of individuals, teams, and organizations. Our capabilities include a wide range of programs, assessments, games, activities, and simulations that address the challenges of today's business community, from coaching and communication, to team building, leadership, and more.

INTRODUCTION

The *Learning Styles Questionnaire* (LSQ) and accompanying interpretive booklet have been written as a result of the work the authors have carried out over a number of years. It is common experience that if two people with the same needs are given the same learning activity, one will learn a lot, the other a little. We think that everyone can learn more effectively when they understand how to use their learning strengths.

This booklet has been written for the learner, irrespective of rank, function, or age. It is assumed that you have already completed and scored the Questionnaire and want to know how to proceed from that point. The following information will help you to make sense of your LSQ results, show you how to select activities that suit your style, and suggest ways to strengthen a style that is currently underdeveloped.

SECTION 1

Understanding Your Learning Styles Questionnaire Results

You should already have completed and scored the LSQ and obtained four scores (ranging from 0—20) for the Activist, Reflector, Theorist, and Pragmatist styles. Because the maximum score for each style is 20, at first sight you might conclude that the highest of your four scores indicates your predominant learning style. However, this is not necessarily so. Before drawing conclusions, you need to view your scores in relation to those obtained by other people who have completed the Questionnaire. Norms have been calculated for various groups of people and you need to decide with which group to compare your scores. If in doubt, use the general norms below, which are based on the scores obtained by more than 3,500 people. The norms are calculated on the scores obtained by:

A. The highest scoring 10% of people.

B. The next 20% of people.

C. The middle 40% of people.

D. The next 20% of people.

E. The lowest scoring 10% of people.

The general norms are as follows:

	A Very Strong Preference	B Strong Preference	C Moderate Preference	D Low Preference	E Very Low Preference
Activist	13 – 20	11 – 12	7 – 10 (mean 9.3)	4 – 6	0 – 3
Reflector	18 – 20	15 – 17	12 – 14 (mean 13.6)	9 – 11	0 – 8
Theorist	16 – 20	14 – 15	11 – 13 (mean 12.5)	8 – 10	0 – 7
Pragmatist	17 – 20	15 – 16	12 – 14 (mean 13.7)	9 – 11	0 – 8

To illustrate how to use norms to interpret your LSQ results let us suppose your scores are Activist 11, Reflector 11, Theorist 11, and Pragmatist 11. We have chosen these scores deliberately because they clearly demonstrate the importance of using norms to reach an interpretation. Based on the norms, a raw score of 11 would relate to each of the styles as follows:

- A score of 11 for Activist falls in the B range indicating a *strong* preference for this style.

- A score of 11 for Reflector falls in the D range indicating a *low* preference for this style.

- A score of 11 for Theorist falls in the C range indicating a *moderate* preference.

- A score of 11 for Pragmatist falls in the D range indicating a *low* preference.

You may prefer to compare your LSQ scores with norms for more specific groups. If so, the next two pages give the norms for eight different groups.

EN-02-NV-07

Salespeople
N = 189

	Activist	Reflector	Theorist	Pragmatist
A	17 – 20	15 – 20	17 – 20	18 – 20
B	15 – 16	12 – 14	14 – 16	16 – 17
C	12 – 14	10 – 11	9 – 13	13 – 15
D	9 – 11	7 – 9	6 – 8	10 – 12
E	0 – 8	0 – 6	0 – 5	0 – 9
Mean	13.3	11.5	11.4	14.1

Research and Development Managers
N = 262

	Activist	Reflector	Theorist	Pragmatist
A	13 – 20	18 – 20	17 – 20	17 – 20
B	10 – 12	16 – 17	15 – 16	15 – 16
C	6 – 9	13 – 15	12 – 14	12 – 14
D	4 – 5	10 – 12	9 – 11	9 – 11
E	0 – 3	0 – 9	0 – 8	0 – 8
Mean	8.0	14.5	13.1	13.4

Trainers
N = 194

	Activist	Reflector	Theorist	Pragmatist
A	16 – 20	19 – 20	17 – 20	17 – 20
B	14 – 15	16 – 18	15 – 16	16 – 16
C	9 – 13	12 – 15	11 – 14	12 – 15
D	7 – 8	8 – 11	7 – 10	10 – 11
E	0 – 6	0 – 7	0 – 6	0 – 9
Mean	10.4	12.4	11.7	12.9

Production Managers
N = 178

	Activist	Reflector	Theorist	Pragmatist
A	12 – 20	17 – 20	19 – 20	19 – 20
B	9 – 11	15 – 16	17 – 18	17 – 18
C	6 – 8	11 – 14	14 – 16	15 – 16
D	3 – 5	7 – 10	12 – 13	12 – 14
E	0 – 2	0 – 6	0 – 11	0 – 11
Mean	7.4	12.7	15.2	16.0

Marketing Managers
N = 93

	Activist	Reflector	Theorist	Pragmatist
A	13 – 20	18 – 20	16 – 20	17 – 20
B	11 – 12	16 – 17	14 – 15	15 – 16
C	7 – 10	12 – 15	10 – 13	13 – 14
D	4 – 6	9 – 11	7 – 9	10 – 12
E	0 – 3	0 – 8	0 – 6	0 – 9
Mean	9.3	13.8	12.5	13.6

Finance Managers
N = 160

	Activist	Reflector	Theorist	Pragmatist
A	10 – 20	19 – 20	18 – 20	18 – 20
B	8 – 9	16 – 18	16 – 17	16 – 17
C	6 – 7	14 – 15	13 – 15	14 – 15
D	3 – 5	10 – 13	11 – 12	11 – 13
E	0 – 2	0 – 9	0 – 10	0 – 10
Mean	7.0	14.9	14.5	15.3

Engineering/Science Graduates
N = 173

	Activist	Reflector	Theorist	Pragmatist
A	13 – 20	18 – 20	16 – 20	16 – 20
B	11 – 12	16 – 17	14 – 15	14 – 15
C	6 – 10	12 – 15	11 – 13	11 – 13
D	4 – 5	9 – 11	8 – 10	9 – 10
E	0 – 3	0 – 8	0 – 7	0 – 8
Mean	8.6	14.2	12.2	12.7

Civil Servants
N = 412

	Activist	Reflector	Theorist	Pragmatist
A	13 – 20	18 – 20	17 – 20	16 – 20
B	9 – 12	16 – 17	15 – 16	15 – 15
C	6 – 8	12 – 15	13 – 14	12 – 14
D	4 – 5	9 – 11	10 – 11	9 – 11
E	0 – 3	0 – 8	0 – 9	0 – 8
Mean	7.7	14.0	13.1	12.7

Students
N = 165

	Activist	Reflector	Theorist	Pragmatist
A	17 – 20	19 – 20	16 – 20	16 – 20
B	15 – 16	17 – 18	14 – 15	14 – 15
C	10 – 14	13 – 16	9 – 13	10 – 13
D	7 – 9	10 – 12	6 – 8	8 – 9
E	0 – 6	0 – 9	0 – 5	0 – 7
Mean	**11.1**	**13.7**	**10.2**	**11.2**

Supervisors
N = 148

	Activist	Reflector	Theorist	Pragmatist
A	16 – 20	19 – 20	17 – 20	18 – 20
B	12 – 15	17 – 18	15 – 16	16 – 17
C	8 – 11	14 – 16	11 – 14	13 – 15
D	6 – 7	11 – 13	9 – 10	11 – 12
E	0 – 5	0 – 10	0 – 8	0 – 10
Mean	**9.7**	**14.6**	**12.2**	**13.1**

Females
N = 117

	Activist	Reflector	Theorist	Pragmatist
A	15 – 20	19 – 20	17 – 20	17 – 20
B	12 – 14	16 – 18	15 – 16	15 – 16
C	8 – 11	12 – 15	12 – 14	12 – 14
D	6 – 7	8 – 11	9 – 11	11 – 11
E	0 – 5	0 – 7	0 – 8	0 – 10
Mean	**9.6**	**12.9**	**12.0**	**13.0**

Males
N = 117

	Activist	Reflector	Theorist	Pragmatist
A	15 – 20	19 – 20	17 – 20	18 – 20
B	12 – 14	17 – 18	16 – 16	17 – 17
C	8 – 11	12 – 16	12 – 15	14 – 16
D	6 – 7	8 – 11	9 – 11	10 – 13
E	0 – 5	0 – 7	0 – 8	0 – 9
Mean	**9.0**	**12.9**	**12.5**	**13.6**

North American Norms

	Activist	Reflector	Theorist	Pragmatist
USA N=862	Mean 9.9	Mean 13.2	Mean 12.8	Mean 13.1
Canada N=46	Mean 8.5	Mean 13.9	Mean 13.6	Mean 14.0

365 Managers Attending IBM Executive Management School (short version)

	Activist	Reflector	Theorist	Pragmatist
France N=51	Mean 10.7	Mean 11.7	Mean 12.7	Mean 14.3
Ger./Aus. N=53	Mean 9.9	Mean 10.8	Mean 11.3	Mean 13.5
Italy N=28	Mean 10.9	Mean 12.0	Mean 13.7	Mean 14.1
Scand. N=44	Mean 12.1	Mean 9.9	Mean 9.9	Mean 13.1
Switz. N=34	Mean 11.8	Mean 11.7	Mean 11.7	Mean 14.8
UK/Ire. N=34	Mean 12.0	Mean 9.3	Mean 10.7	Mean 13.3
USA N=32	Mean 11.5	Mean 10.4	Mean 11.8	Mean 13.9

Questions and Answers

Here are our answers to the questions people most often ask about learning styles, the *Learning Styles Questionnaire,* and the results.

Are there only four learning styles?

Yes. The four styles are a convenient way of describing differences in learning preferences and they reinforce the stages people need to go through in order to be balanced learners. Some researchers have suggested that there are only two learning styles or orientations; *doing* and *thinking.* The doing orientation tends to overlap with a combination of Activist and Pragmatist styles. The thinking orientation overlaps with Reflector and Theorist styles.

Work on brain dominance also suggests that there are two styles; right brain (intuitive, spontaneous, qualitative) and left brain (factual, analytical, quantitative). Right brain dominance tends to overlap with a combination of Activist and Pragmatist styles. Left brain dominance overlaps with Reflector and Theorist styles. More recent theory has divided the brain into four thinking processes (upper and lower left, and upper and lower right).

Can learning style preferences change?

Yes, learning styles, just like any other learned characteristics, are modifiable either at will or by a change of circumstances. Many people have deliberately set out to strengthen underdeveloped styles and thus become more rounded learners (see Sections 4 – 7 of this workbook).

When people change jobs and/or organizations, the altered influences can have an affect on learning styles. Suppose, for example, someone moved from a "quick fix" culture to an organization that by the nature of its work was more reflective. The decrease in the speed of working and the emphasis placed on the painstaking collecting and analysis of data would be likely to increase Reflector/Theorist behavior and, over time, to affect the style preferences. It may well be that a person experiencing such a change would retain their "first love" preferences for Pragmatist/Activist styles. But being forced to use Reflector/Theorist would undoubtedly strengthen the person's repertoire of learning styles.

Similarly, people moving from sales to marketing would be likely to find different occupational learning style preferences. For example, moderate Activists on sales norms would be very strong Activists in a marketing role (unless they deliberately tried to change).

Why do the Questionnaire items probe general behavioral tendencies and not learning?

If you ask people how they learn prior to introducing them to the continuous learning cycle, they will simply say they "just do" and are often incapable of articulating the process they go through. It is more useful, therefore, to ask people questions they can answer that are indirectly indicative of their preferred learning styles. To do so is certainly more helpful (there seems little point in asking people questions they can't answer). The items in the questionnaire also clearly illustrate how learning style preferences underpin, and are associated with, everyday behavioral tendencies. This helps demonstrate the fundamental importance of learning styles.

5

How accurate are self-perceptions?

Accuracy of the LSQ scores usually can be confirmed by people who know the individual in a work context or have shared experiences in training sessions. Views of a domestic partner may differ, as some people behave differently at home.

Sometimes a third party observer of someone's outward behavior may conclude that the person has, for example, Activist preferences. This conclusion might be drawn because people sometimes behave one way while feeling/thinking another. Someone with Reflector preferences may, for example, behave like an Activist because that is expected of him/her or there is pressure to do so. When it comes to likes and dislikes, each individual is best qualified to answer.

However, self-perceptions can be misleading. The LSQ items are easy to sway if someone is determined to give a misleading impression.

Why does the Questionnaire allow only a binary choice ("agree" or "disagree")?

To keep it simple. In the original research we tested a version with a range of answers such as very frequently — frequently — sometimes — infrequently — never. It rendered the same preferences as the simpler version. Therefore, we decided to keep it simple and not complicate the Questionnaire unnecessarily. As a consequence some people feel uncomfortable with being forced to respond one way or the other but they are usually reassured when they understand that the Questionnaire is designed to reveal four *general tendencies* and not a detailed analysis of their whole personality.

Must all the Questionnaire items be answered?

Yes. Items that are left blank might all fall within one learning style and therefore lead to an underestimate of that style.

EN-02-NV-07

What if I don't believe my results?

We suggest you do the following:

1. Check that you still agree with your original responses.

2. Re-examine items that were marginal to see if you have a propensity always to agree or disagree. Decide again on these marginal choices, making sure that you balance your responses.

3. Collect feedback from other people's observations of you either in a training session or at work to see to what extent their perceptions match the Questionnaire results . In our experience the feedback tends to confirm the preferences indicated by the scores. (See Section 8 for suggestions on getting feedback from others.)

Aren't labels misleading/stereotyping?

Like any categorization they are a convenient oversimplification. The styles have to be called *something*; the labels Activist, Reflector, Theorist, and Pragmatist are shorthand. The labels are a starting point for a discussion on how an individual learns.

EN-02-NV-07

SECTION 2

How to Choose Learning Activities That Suit Your Style

Some individuals have a preference for one learning style just as some activities are strongly geared to one style of learning. Where individuals' preferences and the activities to which they are exposed involve the same style, they are likely to learn. If there is a mismatch, they are much less likely to learn. In this section we show how you can make a better choice of activities that are likely to dovetail with your style. We also show activities you may want to avoid, unless you are trying to expand your repertoire of learning styles.

Here are four checklists to help guide you toward learning activities that suit your style. You do not have to study all of them in detail. Just concentrate on the parts that are relevant to you in terms of your LSQ results.

Activists

*If you have a preference for the **Activist Style**, you will learn **best** from activities where:*

- there are *new* experiences/problems/opportunities from which to learn.

- you can engross yourself in short "here and now" activities, such as business games, competitive teamwork tasks, and role playing exercises.

- there is excitement/drama/crisis, things change; there is a range of diverse activities to tackle.

- you have a lot of the limelight/high visibility (you can "chair" meetings, lead discussions, give presentations).

- you are allowed to generate ideas without constraints of policy, structure, or feasibility.

- you are thrown in the deep end with a task you think is difficult (given a challenge with inadequate resources and adverse conditions).

- you are involved with other people, bouncing ideas off them, and solving problems as part of a team.

- it is appropriate to take action.

*As an **Activist** you will learn **least** from activities where:*

- learning involves a passive role (reading, watching, listening to lectures, monologues, explanations, or statements of how things should be done).

- you are asked to stand back and not be involved.

- you are required to assimilate, analyze, and interpret a lot of "messy" data.

- you are required to engage in solitary work (reading, writing, or thinking on your own).

- you are asked to assess beforehand what you will learn, and to appraise afterwards what you have learned.

EN-02-NV-07

- you are offered statements you see as "theoretical," explanations of cause or background.

- you are asked to repeat essentially the same activity over and over again.

- you have precise instructions to follow with little room for maneuvering.

- you are asked to do a thorough job (attend to detail, tie up loose ends, dot the "i's" and and cross the "t's").

Reflector

*If you have a preference for the **Reflector Style**, you will learn **best** from activities where:*

- you are allowed or encouraged to watch/think/mull over activities.

- you are able to stand back from events and listen/observe (observe a group at work, take a back seat in a meeting, watch a film, TV, or video).

- you are allowed to think before acting, to assimilate before commenting (time to prepare, a chance to read in advance a brief giving background data).

- you can carry out some painstaking research (investigate, assemble information, probe to get to the bottom of things).

- you have the opportunity to review what has happened, what you have learned.

- you are asked to produce carefully considered analyses and reports.

- you are helped to exchange views with other people without danger (by prior agreement, within a structured learning experience).

- you can reach a decision in your own time without pressure and tight deadlines.

*As a **Reflector** you will learn **least** from activities where:*

- you are "forced" into the limelight (to act as leader/chairman, to role play in front of onlookers).

- you are involved in situations that require action without planning.

- you are thrown into doing something without warning (forced to react instantly or to produce an off-the-top-of-the-head idea).

- you are given insufficient data on which to base a conclusion.

- you are given cut-and-dried instructions of how things should be done.

- you are worried by time pressures or rushed from one activity to another.

- in the interests of expediency, you have to make shortcuts or do a superficial job.

✎ Theorist

*If you have a preference for the **Theorist Style**, you will learn **best** from activities where:*

♦   what is being offered is part of a system, model, concept, or theory.

♦   you have time to explore methodically the associations and interrelationships between ideas, events, and situations.

♦   you have the chance to question and probe the basic methodology, assumptions, or logic behind something (take part in a question-and-answer session, check a paper for inconsistencies).

♦   you are intellectually stretched (by analyzing a complex situation, being tested in a tutorial session, by teaching high-caliber people who ask searching questions).

♦   you are in structured situations with a clear purpose.

♦   you can listen to or read about ideas and concepts that emphasize rationality or logic and are well-argued/elegant/watertight.

♦   you can analyze and then generalize the reasons for success or failure.

♦   you are offered interesting ideas and concepts, even though they are not immediately relevant.

♦   you are required to understand and participate in complex situations.

*As a **Theorist** you will learn **least** from activities where:*

♦   you are pushed into doing something without a context or apparent purpose.

♦   you have to participate in situations emphasizing emotions and feelings.

♦   you are involved in unstructured activities where ambiguity and uncertainty are high (with open-ended problems, or sensitivity training).

♦   you are asked to act or decide without a basis in policy, principle, or concept.

♦   you are faced with a hodgepodge of alternative or contradictory techniques or methods without exploring any in depth, as in a "once over lightly" course.

♦   you doubt that the subject matter is methodologically sound, where questionnaires have not been validated, where there are not statistics to support an argument.

♦   you find the subject matter platitudinous, shallow, or gimmicky.

♦   you feel yourself out of tune with other participants (when with a lot of Activists or with people of lower intellectual caliber).

✎ Pragmatist

*If you have a preference for the **Pragmatist Style**, you will learn **best** from activities where:*

- there is an obvious link between the subject matter and a problem or opportunity on the job.

- you are shown techniques for doing things with obvious practical advantages (how to save time, how to make a good first impression, how to deal with awkward people).

- you have the chance to try out and practice techniques with coaching/feedback from a credible expert, someone who is successful and can do the techniques him- or herself.

- you are exposed to a model you can emulate (a respected boss, a demonstration from someone with a proven track record, a lot of examples/anecdotes, a film showing how it is done).

- you are given techniques currently applicable to your own job.

- you are given immediate opportunities to implement what you have learned.

- there is high face validity in the learning activity (a good simulation, "real" problems).

- you can concentrate on practical issues (drawing up action plans with an obvious end product, suggesting shortcuts, giving tips).

*As a **Pragmatist** you will learn **least** from activities where:*

- the learning is not related to an immediate need you recognize (you cannot see an immediate or relevant practical benefit).

- organizers of the learning, or the event itself, seem distant from reality ("ivory towered," all theory and general principles, pure "chalk and talk").

- there is no opportunity for practice or clear guidelines on how to perform the activity.

- you feel that people are going around in circles and not getting anywhere fast.

- there are political, managerial, or personal obstacles to implementation.

- there is not apparent reward from the learning activity (more sales, shorter meetings, higher bonus, promotion).

We hope these checklists will help to guide you toward suitable learning experiences. These experiences could include attending a course, seminar, or conference; taking part in a workshop; participating in a project; tackling a special assignment; and so on.

Selecting Learning Activities

Perhaps the most common learning experience likely to come your way is a training event of some kind. Unfortunately, course descriptions are rarely explicit about learning styles, and it is necessary to interpret what they provide from the way the teaching methods are described. This interpretation would best be done either by a direct discussion between you and the course staff, or by asking an adviser within your organization his or her interpretation. Depending on your style preferences, here are some key questions that you should ask before deciding to attend an educational event (or before engaging in any learning activity).

✎ Key Questions for Activists

Will I learn something new that I did not know/could not do before?

Will there be a wide variety of different activities? (I do not want to sit and listen for more than an hour at a stretch!)

Will it be OK to get involved/-"let my hair down"/make mistakes/have fun?

Will I encounter some tough problems and challenges?

Will there be other like-minded people with whom to mix?

Will I have the opportunity to do something?

✎ Key Questions for Reflectors

Will I be given adequate time to consider, assimilate, and prepare?

Will there be opportunities/facilities to assemble relevant information?

Will there be opportunities to listen to other people's points of view — preferably a wide cross-section of people with a variety of views?

Will I be under pressure to be slap-dash or to improvise?

Will there be opportunities to watch other people in action?

EN-02-NV-07

Key Questions for Theorists

Will there be a lot of opportunities to question?

Do the objectives and program of events indicate a clear structure and purpose?

Will I encounter complex ideas and concepts that are likely to stretch me?

Are the approaches to be used and concepts to be explored "respectable," i.e., sound and valid?

Will this experience give me the chance to develop a general view or model?

Key Questions for Pragmatists

Will there be ample opportunities to practice and experiment?

Will there be a lot of practical tips and techniques?

Will we be addressing *real* problems that will result in action plans to tackle some of my current problems?

Will we be exposed to experts who know how to/can do it themselves?

Will this really contribute to the immediate performance of myself and my colleagues?

These questions for each style are worth asking whenever you have the opportunity to ask the organizers of the learning activity. If you are unhappy with the answers and if the proposed course does not seem likely to suit your style, we suggest you search out something that will. However, you may choose to use the activity consciously as a way to improve the range of your learning preferences.

SECTION 3

Making Best Use of Your Learning Strengths

So far we have shown how you can interpret your existing learning styles and make use of that knowledge in selecting learning activities. Because learning is about improving knowledge, skills, and performance, in this section we go further and suggest how you could take greater advantage of opportunities that dovetail with your style. In subsequent sections we suggest how you can build further by tackling the more difficult task of developing your underutilized learning styles.

Learning Opportunities

It is particularly important to emphasize the range of learning opportunities that exist beyond what people learn from a workshop, from a book, or from experience. We distinguish between formal and informal opportunities (though, of course, some opportunities can be either). Some examples are:

Formal Opportunities	**Informal Opportunities**
(activities designed for learning)	(activities that have not been specially designed as learning experiences)
Being coached	Being involved in a major change
Being counseled	Committee meetings
Seminars/workshops/courses	Domestic life
Having a mentor	Familiar tasks
Job rotation	Interactions with people
Reading (as part of a course)	Network contacts
Special projects	Normal work
Stretched boundaries to your job	Problem solving with colleagues
Task groups	Professional meetings
	Projects
	Sporting clubs
	Taking on different work/a new job
	Task groups
	Visiting another organization
	Volunteer work
	Working in a different culture

Developing your existing style may involve first recognizing that you are not making full use of the opportunities available to you; very few people do! Typically, on-the-job learning opportunities far exceed off-the-job learning. Most importantly, on-the-job learning is "real" and you avoid the problem of having to transfer what has been learned.

EN-02-NV-07

Building From Opportunities

While the first step is to look at the general list of opportunities, the second step is to use the questions listed in the previous section to test the possible content of the opportunity. How could the opportunity be used in a way that matches your style? For example:

♦ If I am asked to attend a meeting for the first time, how can I learn from the experience? If I am a strong Reflector, will there be plenty of behavior to observe? How will I collect the information?

♦ If I work for a new manager, and I am a strong Theorist, can I get my manager to talk about the reasons behind the systems and methods he or she uses?

♦ If I am attending a seminar, what kind of learning is involved? Can I get more from it by looking at the behaviors of different people? Why is one facilitator more successful than another? Which of my fellow participants seem to be learning the most and why?

Planning to Learn

Recognition of a learning opportunity is a crucial step. The attempt to see a learning opportunity in terms of its match with your style will help ensure that you use the opportunity efficiently. However, a learning experience is only fully effective when the main stages in the learning process have been planned and followed. This converts a learning opportunity into a learning experience.

Effective learning involves a complete sequence or cycle. Each stage is important not only in achieving completeness, but because each improves learning in the next stage of the cycle.

Our view on learning from experience is that the learning cycle involves:

Experiencing	doing something
Reviewing	thinking about what has happened
Concluding	drawing some conclusions
Planning	deciding what to do in a similar situation

The association between the learning cycle and learning styles is shown below:

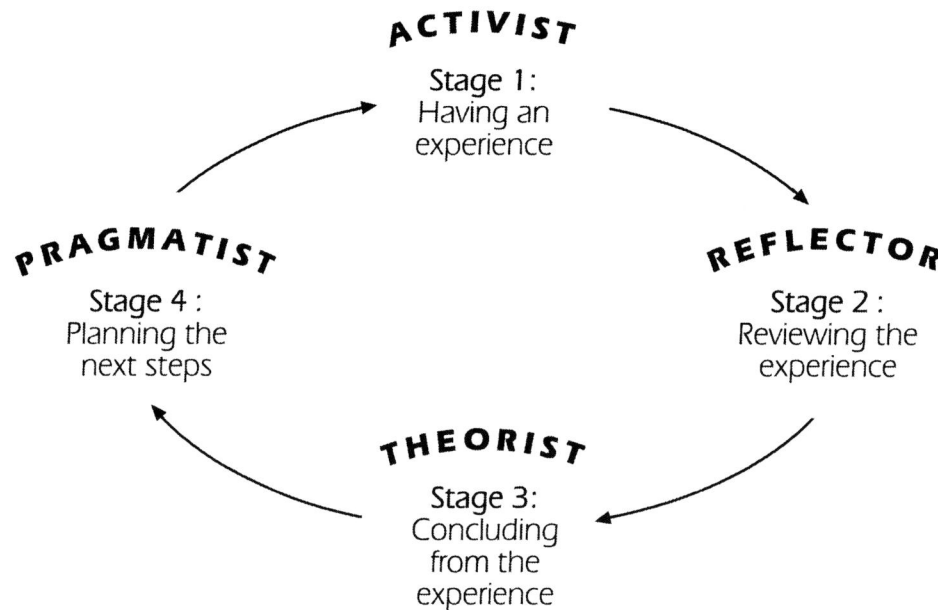

ACTIVIST
Stage 1:
Having an
experience

REFLECTOR
Stage 2 :
Reviewing the
experience

THEORIST
Stage 3:
Concluding
from the
experience

PRAGMATIST
Stage 4 :
Planning the
next steps

If your LSQ results show that you are already a well-balanced learner (i.e., no single style predominates — all four styles are virtually equal), you are likely to manage each stage of this process consciously and well. Your Activist tendencies will ensure that you have plenty of experiences. Your Reflector and Theorist tendencies will ensure that afterwards you review and reach conclusions. Your Pragmatist tendencies will ensure that you plan future implementation.

But what should you do if you have a strong preference for one style? You must make the best use of the strengths of that style, but if you want to be fully equipped to learn from experience you will need to develop styles which at present you do not use. The next four sections provide advice on how to do this. However, *you need not read all four sections.* It is best to concentrate on the section, or sections, that show how to strengthen the style(s) for which your LSQ results indicate you have a low preference. After you have looked at your low or moderate preferences, you might benefit from looking at preferences which are already strong to see how to make them even better.

SECTION 4

How to Improve Your Activist Style

If you want to improve your Activist style because your Activist score was 10 or less, the first task is to decide what aspects you would like to develop. A useful starting point is to do an analysis of the Activist LSQ items where you circled an *X*. These items indicate things you do not do or believe in, and therefore represent opportunities for change or improvement. Identify the items below for which you circled an *X* on the Scoring Form, by circling the item number.

1. I often act without considering the possible consequences.
2. I believe that formal procedures and policies restrict people.
9. I often find that actions based on feelings are as sound as those based on careful thought and analysis.
10. I actively seek out new experiences.
17. I enjoy being the one who talks a lot.
18. I thrive on the challenge of tackling something new and different.
25. I enjoy fun-loving, spontaneous people.
26. I tend to be open about how I am feeling.
33. I prefer to respond to events on a spontaneous, flexible basis rather than plan things out in advance.
34. Quiet, thoughtful people tend to make me feel uneasy.
41. It is more important to enjoy the present moment than to think about the past or future.
42. In discussions I usually produce a lot of spontaneous ideas.
49. More often than not, rules are there to be broken.
50. On balance I talk more than I listen.
57. I am attracted more to novel, unusual ideas than to practical ones.
58. When things go wrong, I am happy to shrug it off and "put it down to experience."
65. I find the formality of having specific objectives and plans stifling.
66. I am usually one of the people who puts life into a party.
73. I quickly get bored with methodical, detailed work.
74. I enjoy the drama and excitement of a crisis situation.

Of the items you *circled*, indicate which are:

> **R** — *rarely* like you
> **S** — *sometimes* like you, but only in specific situations

Mark the above circled items *R* or *S* accordingly.

Now decide which items you want most to practice in order to develop your Activist style. It might be sensible to start with some of the S items because these will be easier to tackle and meet with success. Whether you choose to go for R or S items, or a mixture of the two, we strongly recommend that you focus on a maximum of *three* items. If you aim for more, it is likely to prove too ambitious. The three items you select are best converted into your own words rather than merely copying the original LSQ wording. For example, with item 10, you could write: *I will make an effort to try new things.*

Write the items you most want to develop in the space below.

You have now, in effect, set your objectives. The next step is to commit yourself to some actions that will give you practice in developing your Activist style. Before planning these actions, it is best to take account of the blockages that are currently inhibiting you from being more of an Activist. Common blockages include:

- ◆ fear of failure and of making mistakes
- ◆ fear of ridicule
- ◆ anxiety about trying new or unfamiliar things
- ◆ strong wish to have things well-thought-out in advance
- ◆ self-doubt; lack of self-confidence
- ◆ taking life very seriously/very earnestly.

The actions you plan to improve your Activist style must be feasible rather than "pie in the sky" and specific rather than general. The plans are a commitment to encourage you to do something that you do not normally do. Feasibility and specificity help to ensure that the plan will be successful in prodding you into action. Clearly, you are more likely to take action if you avoid thinking yourself into the deep end. If you are a beginner, it is best to start in the shallow end and graduate to deeper water. Depending on your starting point, some of the suggestions that follow might strike you as too ambitious. If so, you may want to break them down into smaller, more manageable steps. Because your development plans need to be tailor-made to suit your circumstances, we can only offer a variety of suggestions in the hope that they act as useful thought-starters. Here then are a few ideas for strengthening the Activist style.

- ◆ At least once each week, do something that you have never done before: commute to work with a neighbor or coworker; visit a part of your organization that you have neglected; go jogging at lunch time; wear something outrageous to work one day; read an unfamiliar newspaper with views that are diametrically opposed to yours; change the layout of furniture in your office, etc.

- ◆ Practice initiating conversations (especially small talk) with strangers. Select people at random from your organization's telephone directory and talk with them. At large gatherings, conferences, or parties, force yourself to initiate and sustain conversations with *everyone* present. In your spare time go door-to-door canvassing for a cause of your choice.

EN-02-NV-07

- Deliberately fragment your day by taking a break and changing activities every half hour. Make the switch as diverse as possible. For example, if you have had a half hour of cerebral activity, switch to doing something utterly routine and mechanical. If you have been sitting down, stand up. If you have been talking, keep quiet, and so on.

- Force yourself into the limelight. Volunteer whenever possible to chair meetings or give presentations. When you attend a meeting, give yourself the challenge of making a substantial contribution within 10 minutes of the start of the meeting. Get on a soapbox and make a speech at a local event.

- Practice thinking aloud and on your feet. Give yourself a problem and bounce ideas off a colleague (see if you can generate 50 ideas between you in 10 minutes). Get some colleagues/friends to join in a game where you give each other topics and have to give an impromptu speech lasting at least 5 minutes.

SECTION 5
How to Improve Your Reflector Style

If you want to improve your Reflector style because your Reflector score was 14 or less, the first task is to decide what aspects you would like to develop. A useful starting point is to do an analysis of the Reflector LSQ items where you circled an X. These items indicate things you do not do or believe in, and therefore represent opportunities for change or improvement. Identify the items below for which you circled an X on the Scoring Form, by circling the item number.

3. I like the type of work where I have time for thorough preparation and implementation.
4. I listen to other people's points of view before putting my own forward.
11. I take care with the interpretation of data available to me and avoid jumping to conclusions.
12. In discussions I enjoy watching the maneuverings of the other participants.
19. I pay meticulous attention to detail before coming to a conclusion.
20. I am always interested in finding out what people think.
27. I prefer to have as many sources of information as possible — the more data to think over, the better.
28. I take pride in doing a thorough job.
35. I like to reach a decision carefully after weighing many alternatives.
36. It worries me if I have to rush a piece of work to meet a tight deadline.
43. I often get irritated with people who want to rush things.
44. I think that decisions based on a thorough analysis of all the information are sounder than those based on intuition.
51. I prefer to stand back from a situation and consider all the perspectives.
52. I tend to discuss specific things with people rather than to engage in social discussion.
59. If I have a report to write I tend to produce a lot of drafts before settling on the final version.
60. I like to ponder many alternatives before making up my mind.

EN-02-NV-07

67. In discussions I am more likely to adopt a "low profile" than to take the lead and do most of the talking.

68. It is best to think carefully before taking action.

75. On balance I do the listening rather than the talking.

76. I am careful not to jump to conclusions too quickly.

Of the items you *circled*, indicate which are:

    R — *rarely* like you

    S — *sometimes* like you, but only in specific situations

Mark the above circled items *R* or *S* accordingly.

Now decide which items you most want to practice in order to develop your Reflector style. It might be sensible to start with some of the S items because these will be easier to tackle and meet with success. Whether you choose to go for R or S items, or a mixture of the two, we strongly recommend that you focus on a maximum of *three* items. If you aim for more, it is likely to prove too ambitious. The three items you select are best converted into your own words rather than merely copying the original LSQ wording. For example, with item 75, you could write: *I will try to really listen when talking with others.*

Write the items you most want to develop in the space below.

You have now, in effect, set your objectives. The next step is to commit yourself to some actions that will give you practice in developing your Reflector style. Before planning these actions, it is best to take account of the blockages that are currently inhibiting you from being more of a Reflector. Common blockages include:

-    being short of time to plan or think
-    preferring to move quickly from one activity to another
-    being impatient for action
-    a reluctance to listen carefully and analytically
-    a reluctance to write things down.

The actions you plan to improve your Reflector style must be feasible rather than "pie in the sky" and specific rather than general. The plans are a commitment to encourage you to do something that you do not normally do. Feasibility and specificity help to ensure that the plan will be successful in prodding you into action. Clearly, you are more likely to take action if you avoid flinging yourself into the deep end. If you are a beginner, it is best to start in the shallow end and graduate to deeper water. Depending on your starting point, some of the suggestions that follow might strike you as too ambitious. If so, you may want to break them down into smaller, more manageable steps. Because your development plans need to be tailor-made to suit your circumstances, we can only offer a variety of suggestions in the hope that they act as useful thought-starters. Here then are a few ideas for strengthening the Reflector style.

- Practice observing, especially at meetings where there are agenda items that do not involve you directly. Study people's behavior. Keep records about who does the most talking, who interrupts whom, what triggers disagreements, how often the chairman summarizes, and so on. Also study nonverbal behavior. When do people lean forward and lean back? Count how many times people emphasize a point with a gesture. When do people fold their arms, look at their watches, chew their pencils, and so on?

- Keep a diary and each evening write an account of what happened during the day. Reflect on the day's events and see if you can reach any conclusions from them. Record your conclusions in the diary.

- Practice reviewing after a meeting or event of some kind. Go back over the sequence of events identifying what went well and what could have gone better. If possible, tape-record some conversations and play back the tape at least twice, reviewing what happened in great detail. List lessons learned from this activity.

- Give yourself something to research, something that requires the painstaking gathering of data from different sources. Go to your local library and spend a few hours in the reference section.

- Practice producing highly polished pieces of writing. Give yourself essays to write on various topics (something you have researched). Write a report or paper about something. Draft watertight policy statements, agreements, or procedures. When you have written something, put it aside for a week, then force yourself to return to it and do a substantial rewrite.

- Practice drawing up lists for and against a particular course of action. Take a contentious issue and produce balanced arguments from both points of view. Whenever you are with people who want to rush into action, caution them to consider alternatives and to anticipate the consequences.

SECTION 6
How to Improve Your Theorist Style

If you want to improve your Theorist style because your Theorist score was 13 or less, the first task is to decide what aspects you would like to develop. A useful starting point is to do an analysis of the Theorist LSQ items where you circled an X. These items indicate things you do not do or believe in, and therefore represent opportunities for change or improvement.

Identify the items below for which you circled an *X* on the Scoring Form, by circling the item number.

5. I have strong beliefs about what is right and wrong, good and bad.

6. I tend to solve problems using a step-by-step approach.

13. I regularly question people about their basic assumptions.

14. I practice self-discipline such as watching my diet, getting regular exercise, sticking to a fixed routine, etc.

21. I get along best with logical, analytical people and less well with spontaneous, "irrational" people.

22. I do not like disorganized things and prefer to fit things into a coherent pattern.

29. I like to relate my actions to a general principle.

30. I tend to have distant, rather formal relationships with people at work.

37. I believe that rational, logical thinking should win the day.

38. Flippant people who do not take things seriously enough usually irritate me.

45. I tend to be a perfectionist.

46. I can often see inconsistencies and weaknesses in other people's arguments.

53. I find it difficult to produce ideas on impulse.

54. I prefer to reach answers via a logical approach.

61. In discussions with people I often find I am the most dispassionate and objective.

62. I like to be able to relate current actions to a longer-term, bigger picture.

69. I tend to be tough on people who find it difficult to adopt a logical approach.

70. I prefer exploring the basic assumptions, principles, and theories underpinning things and events.

77. I like meetings to be run methodically, sticking to laid down agenda, etc.

78. I steer clear of subjective or ambiguous topics.

Of the items you *circled*, indicate which are:

> **R** — *rarely* like you
>
> **S** — *sometimes* like you, but only in specific situations

Mark the above circled items *R* or *S* accordingly.

Now decide which items you want most to practice in order to develop your Theorist style. It might be sensible to start with some of the S items because these will be easier to tackle and meet with success. Whether you choose to go for R or S items, or a mixture of the two, we strongly recommend that you focus on a maximum of *three* items. If you aim for more, it is likely to prove too ambitious. The three items you select are best converted into your own words rather than merely copying the original LSQ wording. For example, with item 6, you could write: *I will work at developing step-by-step plans to solve problems.*

Write the items you most want to develop in the space below.

```



```

You have now, in effect, set your objectives. The next step is to commit yourself to some actions that will give you practice in developing your Theorist style. Before planning these actions, it is best to take account of the blockages that are currently inhibiting you from being more of a Theorist. Common blockages include:

- taking things at face value
- a preference for intuition and subjectivity
- a dislike of a structured approach to life
- giving high priority to fun loving/spontaneity.

The actions you plan to improve your Theorist style must be feasible rather than "pie in the sky" and specific rather than general. The plans are a commitment to encourage you to do something that you do not normally do. Feasibility and specificity help to ensure that the plan will be successful in prodding you into action. Clearly, you are more likely to take action if you avoid flinging yourself into the deep end. If you are a beginner, it is best to start in the shallow end and graduate to deeper water. Depending on your starting point, some of the suggestions that follow might strike you as too ambitious. If so, you may want to break them down into smaller, more manageable steps. Because your development plans need to be tailor-made to suit your circumstances, we can only offer a variety of suggestions in the hope that they act as useful thought-starters. Here then are a few ideas for strengthening the Theorist style.

- Read something "heavy" and thought-provoking for at least 30 minutes each day. Try philosophy, especially linguistic analysis, logic, or the theory of relativity. If this seems a tall order, try tackling a textbook on management. Whatever you elect to read, try to summarize afterwards what you have read in your own words.

- Practice spotting inconsistencies/weaknesses in other people's arguments. Go through reports, highlighting inconsistencies. Analyze organization charts to discover overlaps and conflicts. Take two newspapers of different persuasions and regularly do a comparative analysis of the differences in their points of view.

- Take a complex situation and analyze it to pinpoint why it developed the way it did, what could have been done differently and at what stage. The situations could be historical, something drawn from current affairs, or something you have been involved in personally. You could, for example, do a detailed analysis of how you spend your time, or of the work flow in and out of your department, or of all the people you interact with and with what frequency in the course of your work.

EN-02-NV-07

- Collect other people's theories, hypotheses, and explanations about events. They might be about environmental issues, theology, the natural sciences, human behavior —*anything*, providing it is a topic with many different, and preferably contradictory, theories. Try to understand the underlying assumptions each theory is based upon and see if you can group similar theories together.

- Practice structuring situations so that they are orderly and more certain to proceed in the way you predict. You might, for example, plan a conference where delegates are going to work in different groupings. Structure the timetable, the tasks, the total-group sessions. Or try structuring a meeting by having a clear purpose, an agenda, and a planned beginning, middle, and end. Invent procedures to cope with problems such as too many people speaking at once or failures to reach a consensus.

- Practice asking probing questions — the type of questions that get to the bottom of things. Refuse to be put off with platitudes or vague answers. Particularly ask questions designed to find out precisely why something has occurred: "Why do you think the machine has gone down again?" "Why is absenteeism increasing?" "Why do more women smoke than men?" "What is the relationship between this problem and what happened last week?"

SECTION 7
How to Improve Your Pragmatist Style

If you want to improve your Pragmatist style because your Pragmatist score was 14 or less, the first task is to decide what aspects you would like to develop. A useful starting point is to do an analysis of the Pragmatist LSQ items where you circled an *X*. These items indicate things you do not do or believe in, and therefore represent opportunities for change or improvement. Identify the items below for which you circled an *X* on the Scoring Form, by circling the item number.

7. I have a reputation for saying what I think, simply and directly.

8. What matters most is whether something works in practice.

15. When I hear about a new idea or approach, I immediately start working out how to apply it in practice.

16. I accept and stick to laid down procedures and policies as long as I regard them as an efficient way of getting the job done.

23. In discussions I like to get straight to the point.

24. I prefer to try things out to see if they work in practice.

31. I tend to be attracted to techniques such as network analysis, flowcharts, branching programs, contingency planning, etc.

32. I tend to judge people's ideas on their practical merits.

39. In meetings I put forward practical, realistic ideas.

40. I can often see better, more practical ways to get things done.

47. I think written reports should be short and to the point.

EN-02-NV-07

48. I like people who approach things realistically rather than theoretically.

55. In discussions I get impatient with irrelevancies and digressions.

56. I believe in coming to the point immediately.

63. I do whatever is expedient to get the job done.

64. I tend to reject wild, spontaneous ideas as being impractical.

71. Most times I believe the end justifies the means.

72. I do not mind hurting people's feelings as long as the job gets done.

79. In discussions I often find I am the realist, keeping people to the point and avoiding wild speculations.

80. People often find me insensitive to their feelings.

Of the items *circled*, indicate which are:

    R — *rarely* like you

    S — *sometimes* like you, but only in specific situations

Mark the above circled items *R* or *S* accordingly.

Now decide which items you want most to practice in order to develop your Pragmatist style. It might be sensible to start with some of the S items because these will be easier to tackle and meet with success. Whether you choose to go for R or S items, or a mixture of the two, we strongly recommend that you focus on a maximum of *three* items. If you aim for more, it is likely to prove too ambitious. The three items you select are best converted into your own words rather than merely copying the original LSQ wording. For example, with item 24, you could write: *I will try an idea out in practice before committing to it.*

Write the items you most want to develop in the space below.

You have now, in effect, set your objectives. The next step is to commit yourself to some actions that will give you practice in developing your Pragmatist style. Before planning these actions, it is best to take account of the blockages that are currently inhibiting you from being more of a Pragmatist. Common blockages include:

♦   a preference for perfect (rather than practical) solutions to problems

♦   seeing even useful techniques as oversimplifications or gimmicky

♦   enjoying interesting diversions (and being side-tracked)

♦   leaving things open-ended rather than committing to specific action

♦   believing that someone else's ideas will not work in your situation.

The actions you plan to improve your Pragmatist style must be feasible rather than "pie in the sky" and specific rather than general. The plans are a commitment to encourage you to do something that you do not normally do. Feasibility and specificity help to ensure that the plan will be successful in prodding you into action. Clearly, you are more likely to take action if you avoid flinging yourself into the deep end. If you are a beginner, it is best to start in the shallow end and graduate to deeper water. Depending on your starting point, some of the suggestions that follow might strike you as too ambitious. If so, you may want to break them down into smaller, more manageable steps. Because your development plans need to be tailor-made to suit your circumstances, we can only offer a variety of suggestions in the hope that they act as useful thought-starters. Here then are a few ideas for strengthening the Pragmatist style.

♦ Collect techniques — practical ways of doing things. The techniques can be about anything potentially useful to you. They might be analytical techniques such as critical path analysis or cost benefit analysis. They might be interpersonal techniques such as Transactional Analysis, or assertiveness or presentation techniques. They might be time-saving techniques, statistical techniques, techniques to improve your memory, or techniques to cope with stress and reduce your blood pressure.

♦ In meetings and discussions of any kind (progress meetings, problem-solving meetings, planning meetings, appraisal discussions, negotiations, sales calls, etc.), concentrate on producing action plans. Make it a rule never to emerge from a meeting or discussion without a list of actions either for yourself, for others, or both. The action plans should be specific and include a deadline (e.g., "I will produce Chapter 4 by May 31." "Bill will produce a two-page paper listing alternative bonus schemes by Sept. 1.").

♦ Make opportunities to experiment with some of your newfound techniques. Try them out in practice. If your experiment involves other people, then tell them openly that you are conducting an experiment and explain the technique which is about to be tested. (This reduces embarrassment in the event the technique is a flop.) Choose the time and place for your experiments. Avoid situations where a lot is at stake and where the risks of failure are unacceptably high. Experiment in routine settings with people whose aid or support you can enlist.

♦ Study techniques that other people use and then model yourself on them. Pick up techniques from your manager, your manager's manager, your colleagues, your employees, visiting salespeople, interviewers on television, politicians, actors and actresses, or your next-door neighbor. When you discover something they do well — emulate them. Subject yourself to scrutiny from "experts" so that they can watch your technique and coach you in how to improve it. Invite someone who is skilled in running meetings to sit in and watch you chairing; get an accomplished presenter to give you feedback on your presentation techniques. The idea is to solicit help from people who have a proven track record — it is the equivalent of having a coaching session with a golfing professional.

♦ Tackle a "do-it-yourself" project — it does not matter if you are not good with your hands. Pragmatists are practical and, if only for practice purposes, D.I.Y. activities help to develop a practical outlook. Renovate a piece of furniture, build a garden shed, or even an extension to your house. At work calculate your own statistics once in a while instead of relying on a printout; be your own organization and methods consultant; go to visit the shop floor in search of practical problems to solve. Learn to type; learn a foreign language.

SECTION 8

Getting Help From Others

Help from other people is potentially available at four stages:

♦ when you have completed and scored your LSQ and want to check whether other people have the same perception of your approach to learning

♦ when you want to make decisions about the kind of learning activities you should seek

♦ when you want to get feedback on how you are using learning opportunities

♦ when you want to get coaching on what you are doing.

Checking Your LSQ Score

It is sensible after scoring your LSQ to ask someone else whether they see your approach to learning in the same way. You will probably only want to do this if you have doubts about your results and would welcome a second opinion.

Obviously, the checking process is best done by someone who knows you well and knows the basis for the LSQ, but the latter is not essential. The most detailed and useful approach is to ask someone to take the LSQ *about you*. If there are substantial differences in your perceptions, as shown in the total scores, then it is worth going over the individual questions to check the differences in detail and the reasons for them.

If the relationship between you and your manager makes it feasible, it would be best to ask him or her to do this. You may be more comfortable in asking a colleague to help you. You could ask your spouse to check the results, although there may be differences in your behavior at home, which could explain possible differences in the way your spouse sees you.

Deciding on Learning Activities

As we have shown in Sections 2 and 3, your LSQ results can be used to help you choose which learning activities to undertake. Your manager and/or training adviser could assist you with this in two ways. They could help to check that any association you make between your style and a learning activity is accurate. Secondly, they could help to point you in the direction of opportunities that could make use of your strengths or assist you in working on your weaknesses.

EN-02-NV-07

Feedback on Using Learning Opportunities

It is important to monitor the way in which you learn from chosen activities. As in much else in life, the distance between planning to do something and actually achieving it can be substantial.

The role of helpers can be to encourage you to do your own monitoring and give you feedback on what they see occurring while you are learning. You also can ask your manager or colleagues to provide you with feedback in your normal work situation. In this context, however, you should be selective because neither manager nor colleagues will welcome being asked to monitor you constantly. You should be specific in asking them to watch for particular things. They should not be asked, "How well do you think I am learning?" Ask instead, "What did you think about my response to that situation? Did I . . . ?"

Getting Coaching from Others

We have deliberately separated this from seeking feedback, although often the two will seem to accompany each other naturally. We think it is more helpful to see the two as separate because the capacity to give accurate feedback is not necessarily accompanied by the ability to give good advice. It may be sensible to go to a different colleague or adviser for advice on what to do.

Again, while coaching can be accomplished in a formal learning program, it can also be developed on the job. You may choose to go to a colleague who has particular learning strengths to see how he or she uses those strengths.

Be careful not to discount suggestions from others whose styles are not the same as yours. Differences of style between manager and employee can be turned to advantage and become reciprocally beneficial. The same comment applies to relationships between colleagues and in groups where there are a range of different learning style preferences.

We recognize that some people are reluctant to ask for help. We also know that some people lack the capacity to give help. However, our experience in general is that more people could ask and more could give than currently do so. We have found that an awareness of different learning styles makes it far easier for people to broach the subject and ask for feedback and coaching from those around them. It is up to you to take the initiative in getting help from others.

SECTION 9

Keeping a Learning Log

Learning should not be left to chance. It is best done as a deliberate, conscious process. To aid this, we suggest you develop the habit of keeping a learning log. After you have reviewed your low or moderate preferences, you might benefit from looking at preferences that are already strong to see how to make them even better.

Fundamentally, learning from experience is a four-stage process:

Stage	Most Suited to
1. Having an experience	Activist
2. Reviewing the experience	Reflector
3. Concluding from the experience	Theorist
4. Planning the next steps	Pragmatist

The learning log is especially helpful in carrying out steps 2, 3, and 4. Keeping a log also helps "force" you (if that is what it takes) to search out and take learning opportunities because the discipline of making log entries puts a certain amount of pressure on you to have something to enter.

Each time you use your learning log, we recommend the following procedure:

◆   Start by thinking back over the experience and selecting a part of it to focus on in your log. You might choose something that was significant or important to you. On the other hand, you could choose something that struck you as routine or even mundane. Whatever you choose to focus on, the log invites you to be selective. You don't need to write at length about everything that happened.

◆   Write a detailed account of what happened during that period of the activity. Do not, at this stage, put any effort into deciding what you learned — just concentrate on describing what actually happened.

◆   List the conclusions you have reached as a result of the experience. These are in effect, your learning points. Do not limit the number or worry about the practicality or quality of the points.

◆   Finally, decide which learning points you want to implement in the future and work out an action plan that covers:

  ◆   What you are going to do
  ◆   When you are going to do it.

Spell out your action plan as precisely as possible so that you are clear on what you have to do and can ensure that your plans are realistic.

EN-02-NV-07

It is not necessary to complete every step all at once. You could, for example, write a description of what happened while it is fresh in your mind and at some later stage, after time for reflection, record your conclusions and plan. Even the conclusions and the plan could be recorded at different times. The important thing, however, is eventually to have filled in all three boxes, thus ensuring that you complete all the stages in the learning cycle.

You can design your own learning log, but here are some suggested worksheets.

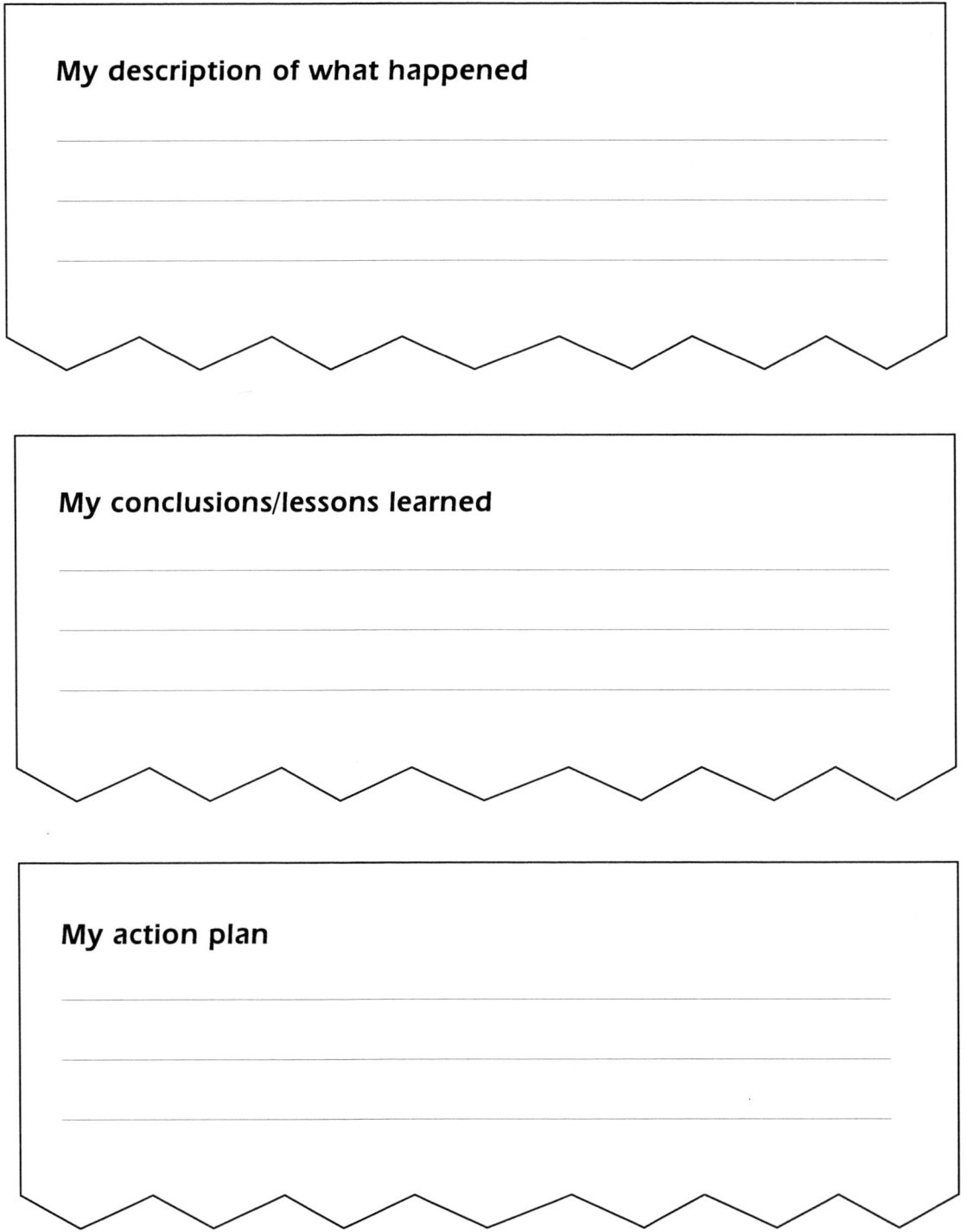

My description of what happened

My conclusions/lessons learned

My action plan

EN-02-NV-07

Welcome to a better way to train.

With the experiential solutions of HRDQ, you'll engage and involve your learners. And research shows that's what makes the difference. According to the NTL Institute for Applied Behavioral Sciences, people remember just half of what they hear in a lecture, while they retain up to 75% if they can "practice by doing."

Building a model with teammates. Taking a skills assessment. Role-playing. Action planning. It's all part of the HRDQ experience. For more than 25 years, we've helped thousands of leading organizations improve performance and solve business challenges with learning solutions based on our unique Experiential Learning Model™. And we want to help you do the same.

" Learning is not a spectator sport. Learners do not learn much by just sitting and listening, memorizing prepackaged assignments, and spitting out answers. They must talk about what they are learning, write about it, relate it to past experiences, apply it to their daily lives. They must make what they learn part of themselves. **"**

A.W. CHICKERING AND Z.F. GAMSON
"SEVEN PRINCIPLES FOR GOOD PRACTICE"
AAHE BULLETIN, 1987

rev 06.07

HRDQ
CLIENT
SOLUTIONS
Team

Call on us today. We'll help you find the right products to match your training needs. 800.633.4533

Capitalizing on Your Learning Style
CODE 1205WB
may be ordered from:

2002 Renaissance Boulevard #100
King of Prussia, PA 19406-2756
800.633.4533 ▪ www.hrdq.com

FOR CANADIAN DISTRIBUTION PLEASE CONTACT:
Organizational Learning Resources
372 Moonstone Rd. E., P.O. Box 268, Moonstone, ON Canada L0K 1N0
Tel: 888-889-2184   Fax: 888-889-2183
www.olresources.ca

EN-02-NV-07